HOMELAND SECURITY AND DEFENSE CENTER

Modeling Terrorism Risk to the Air Transportation System

An Independent Assessment of TSA's Risk Management Analysis Tool and Associated Methods

Andrew R. Morral, Carter C. Price, David S. Ortiz, Bradley Wilson, Tom LaTourrette, Blake W. Mobley, Shawn McKay, Henry H. Willis

Prepared for the Transportation Security Administration

The research described in this report was prepared for the Transportation Security Administration and conducted within the RAND National Defense Research Institute, a federally funded research and development center sponsored by the Office of the Secretary of Defense, the Joint Staff, the Unified Combatant Commands, the Navy, the Marine Corps, the defense agencies, and the defense Intelligence Community under Contract W74V8H-06-C-0002.

Library of Congress Control Number: 2012953351

ISBN: 978-0-8330-7685-4

The RAND Corporation is a nonprofit institution that helps improve policy and decisionmaking through research and analysis. RAND's publications do not necessarily reflect the opinions of its research clients and sponsors.

RAND® is a registered trademark.

Published 2012 by the RAND Corporation
1776 Main Street, P.O. Box 2138, Santa Monica, CA 90407-2138
1200 South Hayes Street, Arlington, VA 22202-5050
4570 Fifth Avenue, Suite 600, Pittsburgh, PA 15213-2665
RAND URL: http://www.rand.org/
To order RAND documents or to obtain additional information, contact
Distribution Services: Telephone: (310) 451-7002;
Fax: (310) 451-6915; Email: order@rand.org

Preface

After several years of discussion with industry about aviation risk management and the operational and economic impact of security measures, the Transportation Security Administration (TSA) concluded in late 2005 that it required a "revolutionary" approach to understanding air transportation risk and the net reductions in risk associated with individual countermeasures. In July 2007, Boeing entered into an agreement with TSA to develop and operate the Risk Management Analysis Tool (RMAT) and associated risk-management processes. These were designed to model and explain the complex interactions between security providers and systems and adversaries hoping to attack the commercial air transportation system.

RMAT is used by TSA to estimate the terrorism risk-reduction benefits attributable to new and existing security programs, technologies, and procedures. For instance, RMAT has been used to estimate the risk-reduction benefits attributable to behavior detection officers, and Advanced Imaging Technology (such as full-body scanners), for purposes of supporting cost-benefit analyses of these programs.

Whereas RMAT has clearly benefitted from the combined expertise and investments of Boeing, TSA, and other industry and governmental stakeholders who have participated in a working group advising on RMAT development, the tool itself is sufficiently complex that it cannot rely on the transparency of its methods to support its face validity.

Before relying on RMAT results for high-stakes resource management and policy decisions, therefore, TSA leadership requested that the

RAND Corporation conduct an independent assessment of the validity of the RMAT terrorism risk model for these purposes. This report describes RAND's approach to this assessment, its results, and recommendations for how TSA and Boeing might further develop and work with RMAT in the future.

This research was sponsored by the Risk and Capabilities Analysis Design office of TSA and was conducted within the RAND Homeland Security and Defense Center, a joint center of RAND Infrastructure, Safety, and Environment and the RAND National Defense Research Institute, a federally funded research and development center sponsored by the Office of the Secretary of Defense, the Joint Staff, the Unified Combatant Commands, the Navy, the Marine Corps, the defense agencies, and the defense Intelligence Community.

For more information on the RAND Homeland Security and Defense Center, and for additional published work on terrorism risk management, see http://www.rand.org/multi/homeland-security-and-defense.html.

Contents

Figure and Tables

Figure

Tables

Summary

To support policy and resource allocation decisions, the Department of Homeland Security (DHS) and the Transportation Security Administration (TSA) have developed a suite of tools and processes for conducting risk assessments. One such tool is the Risk Management Analysis Tool (RMAT) developed by the Boeing Company and TSA in consultation with private sector and governmental members of a risk management working group. In December 2010, TSA asked RAND to evaluate whether RMAT provides results that are valid for TSA's risk-assessment needs. This report describes RAND's approach to this assessment and our findings.

RMAT simulates terrorist behavior and success in attacking vulnerabilities in the domestic commercial air transportation system. In doing so, it draws on estimates of terrorist resources, capabilities, preferences, decision processes, intelligence collection, and operational planning. It describes how the layers of security protecting the air transportation system are likely to perform in the face of a range of more than 60 types of attack. It draws on detailed blast and other physical modeling to understand the damage produced by different weapons and attacks and calculates the direct and indirect economic consequences of that damage. As such, the tool is designed to provide vital information that can help TSA understand the risks to which the entire air transportation system is exposed and develop ways to improve it.

RAND's approach to validating RMAT required first establishing TSA's intended uses and requirements for risk assessment and then evaluating which of those requirements RMAT can satisfy. We have not validated RMAT against a set of original requirements for the system, because RMAT has evolved over time without such a guiding set of requirements. Instead, therefore, we evaluate TSA's current and broad risk-assessment requirements that RMAT can validly support.

We divided the validation effort into four substantive research questions:

1. Are the adversary behavior and air transportation system conceptual models valid, and are the data used to support them adequate? (Chapters Two and Three)
2. Are the sources and methods for populating the RMAT model with data sufficient to ensure their validity? (Chapter Four)
3. Does the RMAT code, as implemented, perform in the way it was designed to? (Chapter Five)
4. Can risk estimates from RMAT be used in the ways TSA intends? (Chapter Six)

These validation efforts considered diverse sources of evidence, including published scientific literature, elicited judgments from subject matter experts, considerations of logic and reasonableness, historical evidence, and quantitative empirical analysis of RMAT and its outputs. Each of these chapters includes detailed observations about RMAT strengths and weaknesses and concludes with a set of recommendations for further developing RMAT. In this Summary, we highlight only the main findings from the study.

RMAT Suitability for TSA Risk Assessment

RMAT is built around two innovative conceptual models: an adversary model that simulates adversary efforts to select, plan for, and execute attacks; and a defender model that simulates how the air transportation system will react to each attack.

As one of the first general theories of terrorism designed to account for adversary resource constraints, intelligence collection, targeting, utility functions, and operations, the RMAT adversary model represents a potentially important contribution to the terrorism research community. Nevertheless, it also necessarily relies on assumptions that are speculative and requires data as inputs that are subject to great uncertainty. As such, we do not believe that the adversary model should be regarded as likely to accurately anticipate terrorist behavior. We do think that it is useful analytically, however, such as for exploring how plausible characteristics and choices of adversaries might affect risk, refining analysts' understanding of the complexity of terrorist behavior, or helping to focus intelligence collection activities on features of terrorist behavior that RMAT identifies as important. Such uses are valuable. Just as with other terrorism risk models we have examined, however, these uses do not include prediction of the most likely actual adversary strategies.

TSA and Boeing recognized the limitations of the adversary model and have adopted strategies for working with RMAT that reduce reliance on it. RMAT can be run in such a way that adversaries are forced to attempt specific attacks, thereby circumventing some more speculative parts of the model that simulate adversary preferences and choice behavior. Even in this mode, however, the adversary must construct a plan, gather intelligence and resources, conduct dry runs, and perform other activities that affect the likelihood of success. Thus, results continue to depend on adversary modeling that is subject to major assumptions and important sources of uncertainty. The assumptions may be reasonable for some adversaries, in which case the results might be quite good. For others, the results may be quite poor. As such, the model results cannot be assumed to reliably anticipate system terrorism risks.

The defender model, which characterizes the U.S. domestic air transportation security system, is a particular strength of RMAT. The current abstract air transportation system modeled in RMAT appears to capture the key features relevant to security at most airports. If we have good information about an adversary's capabilities and intentions, the RMAT defender model can provide credible and useful estimates of the likelihood of detecting and interdicting the adversary. Moreover, modification of the generalized airport configuration is straightforward, so to the extent they fall within the scope of the RMAT "world," new places, processes, and vulnerabilities can be incorporated.

There are some gaps in the defender model that TSA and Boeing should consider remedying, as these limit its scope and validity and could introduce unwanted biases in RMAT results. Chief among these recommended improvements is broadening the scope of the domestic air transportation system to include its interfaces with non-U.S. airports and inbound foreign flights. Additional improvements to this portion of the model may include expanding the range of security threats considered under RMAT, expanding the range of attack pathways available to attackers, and inclusion of off-airport freight processing, catering, general aviation, mass transit, air traffic control, and booking information systems. Some of these recommended changes have already been planned by the RMAT development team.

Both the adversary and the defender models place heavy demands on the identification, validation, and maintenance of the roughly 4,300 input values quantifying aspects of airports, security operations, terrorists, attack outcomes, and their valuations. To fulfill model data requirements, Boeing and TSA have undertaken repeated data collection efforts that have relied on elicitations from subject matter experts; assessments of technical, red-teaming, and scientific data; review of TSA policies and procedures; and other data sources.

In reviewing a sample of RMAT data inputs, the RAND team was able to validate the reasonableness, if not necessarily the real-world correctness, for more than half of the parameter values either on logical grounds (e.g., nonmetallic knives are not explosive and do not contain any metal) or by confirming values through literature searches or consultation with subject matter experts. Nevertheless, some values appeared wrong to us, and others required estimates that call for information that either does not exist or is subject to such profound uncertainty that we judged they should not be estimated as point values but, rather, explicitly treated as ranges and sources of deep uncertainty affecting RMAT estimates. Boeing considers the specific parameters used in the model to be proprietary, so we are prohibited from illustrating this point with examples. Suffice it to say, however, that portions of the model attempt to parameterize quite specific features of terrorists' decision criteria, including specification of their risk tolerance, preferences, knowledge, and learning. Such RMAT variables are important in the model but require precision beyond what intelligence or academic research can credibly provide. Estimating ranges of values is often more plausible, but understanding the implications of these uncertainties on model results should be a priority in future work with the model.

RMAT uses subject matter experts as sources for roughly two-thirds of its input data. After reviewing TSA and Boeing methods for eliciting subject matter expert judgments, we offer several suggestions for improving the elicitation process and results. In addition, we recommend relying less on subject matter expert judgments when scientific or empirical literature is available as relevant input data and expanding the pool of experts used to provide judgments on RMAT conceptual models and parameter values.

To produce valid and useful results, RMAT requires more than just good conceptual models and valid input data; it needs code that faithfully characterizes the conceptual models and change management processes that help ensure that the code remains faithful through periodic modifications necessary for new case studies of risk, when improvements are made to the conceptual model, or when coding errors are corrected. To evaluate the RMAT software, we ran third-party software quality diagnostic tools on its code, we conducted sensitivity analysis experiments to establish whether input and output variables are associated in predictable ways, and we evaluated the change management processes used to maintain the software.

RMAT was originally developed as a prototype, and it has evolved continuously to fit new uses and requirements. The result is a complex program with less organization and efficiency than would be expected of a production model. Given the rapid pace of progress and changing requirements, it is easy to understand the software's current state, but it implies significant challenges for expanding, revising, debugging, testing, and managing the code—all of which threaten its ongoing reliability and validity. Boeing is aware of these code issues, of course, and reports that it is in the process of improving the RMAT source code. Our point here is not to criticize, because such complex and ambitious undertakings often exhibit these types of problems along the way, but to point out that moving forward to something stable, solid, and adaptable will be important but challenging.

Our sensitivity tests found that most, but not all, relationships between inputs and outputs are in the expected direction. Moreover, several relationships we expected to find were not present, such as associations between the probability of successfully entering the flight deck or the probability of air marshals being onboard and either the attractiveness or success of hijack attempts. We allowed the probability of federal air marshals being present on the hijacked aircraft to vary across a wide range, yet the model suggests that their presence or absence has no significant influence over hijack success rates—a result that is hard to understand.

Of the variables that appear most often to have a significant influence on outcomes, many are those we consider to be difficult or impossible to estimate with precision. These include judgments about how much perceived risk might color the decisions of current and future terrorists or how large the maximum possible size of terrorist cells might be when considering known and unknown groups.

These are all parameters that are subject to deep uncertainty and, no doubt, to wide variation across terrorist groups. Subject matter experts and intelligence analysts cannot credibly supply meaningful point estimates of these values. That these parameters also happen to explain a large portion of the variance in RMAT outcomes suggests the need for caution when interpreting model results based on rough estimates for these uncertain parameters.

Finally, our review finds that RMAT is capable of supporting several of TSA's risk-assessment intended uses but that its design is not always conducive to these purposes. TSA must make high-stakes resource allocation decisions designed to counter threats that are not well known, that are continuously evolving, and that may intelligently adapt to circumvent our security measures. This is a complex problem and one for which there may not be one best answer.

A recurring theme in our review is that it is a serious error to imagine that the correct values of all the parameters of a good model such as RMAT can be established. The analytic endeavor should be conceived differently so as to acknowledge the need for exploratory analysis under uncertainty. Because future terrorism risks are subject to sources of deep uncertainty, TSA should not seek security solutions that are optimized for a set of plausible and carefully collected input values. Instead, it should search for solutions that perform well across a range of input values selected to span the space of plausible future conditions. This type of exploratory analysis is invaluable for identifying robust solutions and understanding the conditions under which different solutions might be expected to perform well.

TSA has some procedures in place to explore the implications of key uncertainties. For instance, it uses sensitivity analysis methods to consider how risk reduction might vary with different RMAT assumptions about attacker capabilities, the expected number of attacks per year, or expectable improvements in technology. This approach provides insights into the robustness of the RMAT results to differing assumptions and represents an important advance in TSA approaches to understanding the risks it is charged with managing. But this approach still assumes that many other uncertain variables are estimated accurately.

A better approach, we believe, would use a simplified low-resolution terrorism risk model abstracted from RMAT to highlight the key sources of uncertainty affecting outcomes and then use exploratory analysis to evaluate the space of possible future outcomes using a spanning set of test cases or parameter values for all important and uncertain parameter values and assumptions. A similar approach is now reflected in Department of Defense planning (as in the 2009 *Quadrennial Defense Review*). In this report, we discuss how insights and parameter estimates from the RMAT might be used to support low-resolution models that could provide TSA with transparent analyses of the effects of deep uncertainties on risk and the decisions TSA must make.

Conclusions

RMAT has proven to be of great value to TSA in driving a more sophisticated understanding of terrorism risks to the air transportation system. Indeed, at the time RMAT was begun, TSA's approach to risk analysis and risk management was rudimentary. The process of developing RMAT led TSA to increasingly sophisticated understandings of the nature of terrorism threats, vulnerabilities, and consequences, as demonstrated in its current risk doctrine.

This is an example of one principal value that high-resolution models such as RMAT offer. Specifically, they can be invaluable for facilitating understanding of important phenomena and for recording, structuring, and conveying information that is complex and not well understood. Such models can become essential textbooks for training analysts and leaders to think more clearly and productively about complex phenomena and for driving developments in our theory and conceptual models for these phenomena. RMAT is clearly well suited for such purposes.

In addition, we find that RMAT fully or partially satisfies 16 of TSA's 19 high- and medium-priority risk-assessment requirements, making it a valuable addition to TSA's collection of analytic tools and methods.

As with all other terrorism risk models, however, it is not well suited for revealing how the future is likely to unfold. Even if the conceptual models on which RMAT is built were sound and comprehensive, the input data requirements exceed what subject matter experts or science can estimate with precision, and the imprecision of those estimates is subject to unknown sources and ranges of error. That said, we recommend that TSA make RMAT a component of a new exploratory and multiresolution modeling approach for supporting resource allocation and high-level policy questions.

Acknowledgments

This report benefited from extensive consultation with and cooperation from the Boeing Company's RMAT development team, including Jim Vasatka, Gary Kamsickas, Chris Forgie, Herbert Wilson, Mike Garrett, and William Tucker.

In addition, we are grateful to the insights on risk and TSA risk-assessment requirements offered by Dominic Bianchini, Andrew Cox, Wesley Henderson, Robin Kane, Jennifer King, and Rich Kraske at TSA and by Dawn Riddle, Jennifer LeMoine, and Peter Liu of Deloitte Touche. The project team received valuable industry perspectives on risk from Boeing and from consultations with Randy Harris of Delta Airlines, Eric Thacker of the Air Transport Association, and Chris Bidwell and Lydia Ortiz of the Airports Council International.

We are especially grateful to the subject matter experts who offered their judgments on the validity of model parameters and concepts in those areas for which we could not find authoritative documentation. These experts included Shannon Garcia-Hamilton (TSA), Richard Hoffman (RAND), Julie Kim (RAND), Errol Southers (formerly with the Los Angeles Airport Police Department), Greg Staar (Ontario California Airport Police), and Danny Turner (TSA).

Finally, for important insights on validation of complex models, we thank Robert Anderson, Bart Bennett, and Paul Davis (RAND), Alok Chaturvedi (Simulex Inc.), Erin Fitzgerald (Minerva Research Initiative, Department of Defense [DoD] Basic Science Office), Lee Krause (Securboration), Midh Mulpuri (Simulex Inc.), Stephen Lord (U.S. Government Accountability Office), and Al Sweetser (Simulation and Analysis Center, Office of the Secretary of Defense).

Abbreviations

AIT	Advanced Imaging Technology
AOA	air operations area
AQ	Al-Qa'ida
AQAP	Al-Qa'ida in the Arabian Peninsula
ASAP	Aviation Security Assessment Program
BDO	behavior detection officers
DHS	Department of Homeland Security
DoD	Department of Defense
ETDS	Explosives Trace Detection Systems
GAO	Government Accountability Office
HSI	Homeland Security Institute
MIPT	Memorial Institute for the Prevention of Terrorism
NIPP	National Infrastructure Protection Plan
NOLH	near-orthogonal Latin hypercube
NRC	National Research Council
OMB	Office of Management and Budget
RMAP	risk management analysis processes

RMAT	Risk Management Analysis Tool
RPG	rocket-propelled grenade
SPOT	Screening Passengers by Observational Technique (program)
TSA	Transportation Security Administration
TSO	transportation security officer
TSSRA	Transportation Sector Security Risk Assessment
U.K.	United Kingdom
XML	Extensible Markup Language

CHAPTER ONE

Introduction

In establishing the Department of Homeland Security (DHS) in 2002, Congress directed DHS to develop risk-management principles for protecting critical infrastructure sectors such as transportation. This requirement was elaborated by Homeland Security Presidential Directive 7, the National Infrastructure Protection Plan, and other legislation and policies. These highlighted the importance of developing reliable and valid assessments of security risks that account systematically for the threats, vulnerabilities, and consequences to which transportation systems and other critical infrastructure are exposed.

Early DHS and Transportation Security Administration (TSA) risk-analysis efforts revealed the complexity of critical infrastructure risks when threats involve intelligent adversaries who may adapt to security countermeasures and whose number, location, and intentions are poorly known. Tools such as the Risk Analysis and Management for Critical Asset Protection and TSA's National Transportation Sector Risk Analysis were soon abandoned because of the challenges of accurately measuring key inputs, such as the likelihoods of different attack scenarios and the expected direct and indirect consequences of successful attacks.

These challenges did not relieve TSA or the department of its obligations to perform credible risk assessments. Indeed, the Government Accountability Office (GAO), Office of Management and Budget (OMB), and Congress have continued to press the secretary and the administrator of TSA to justify security priorities in a rational, comprehensive, and transparent way, noting that the alternative of basing decisions chiefly on intelligence assessment of threats is inadequate for ensuring cost-effective security solutions (GAO, 2009).

DHS and TSA have invested in increasingly complex risk models designed, in some cases, to predict terrorist decisionmaking and behavior from first principles, to perform detailed blast and other effect modeling to understand the kinetic effects of different weapons, and to construct sophisticated economic models of the cascading effects of terrorist attacks on local, regional, and national economies.

Inevitably, the added complexity of these newer risk models makes them less transparent than earlier, low-resolution models that worked from rough aggregate estimates of threats, vulnerabilities, and consequences. With the loss of transparency, important questions have been raised about the validity of current terrorism risk models and whether they are sufficiently accurate to be used in homeland security planning. For instance, in its 2010 report on risk modeling at DHS, a National Academy of Sciences panel reported that "with the exception of risk analysis for natural disaster preparedness, the committee did not find any DHS risk-analysis capabilities and methods that are yet adequate for supporting DHS decision making, because their validity and reliability are untested" (National Research Council [NRC], 2010, p. 2). They went on to recommend that "DHS should strengthen its scientific practices, such as documentation, validation, and peer review by technical experts external to DHS. This strengthening of its practices will also contribute greatly to the transparency of DHS's risk modeling and analysis" (p. 3).[1]

In the spirit of this recommendation, TSA asked the RAND Corporation to perform an independent validation of the Risk Management and Analysis Tool (RMAT), a simulation model of terrorism risks faced by the commercial domestic air transportation system.

This report describes our assessment of RMAT assumptions, input data, and model performance but does so in a way designed

---

[1] As discussed later in this report, RAND's view is that the NRC recommendations overstressed "validation" and greatly underemphasized the need to characterize uncertainties and build uncertainty into analysis. Achieving high "accuracy" is sometimes impossible, but good analysis under uncertainty is feasible.

to protect sensitive information about true air transportation vulnerabilities. RMAT assumptions do not represent standard TSA assumptions, and the inputs we used to test RMAT performance were not the security-sensitive inputs used by TSA when using RMAT to evaluate system security. That is, *the assumptions, strengths, weaknesses, and results of RMAT described in this report should not be interpreted to accurately reflect TSA's wider risk-assessment assumptions and estimates, as TSA decisionmakers draw on a range of risk-assessment methods and information in addition to RMAT.*

RMAT and Its Current Use

After several years of discussion with industry about aviation risk management and the operational and economic impact of security measures, TSA concluded in late 2005 that it required a "revolutionary" approach to understanding air transportation risk and the net reductions in risk associated with individual countermeasures. TSA, industry and government stakeholders in aviation security, and Boeing jointly developed a functional analysis of requirements for such a model in February 2006, which described the importance of understanding how adversaries and defenders interact.

Boeing began development of the risk-modeling prototype tool that RMAT evolved from in 2004 and continues to own and operate it at no cost to the U.S. government. Boeing representatives explain the company's investment in the model as reflecting its concern with ensuring the safety and prosperity of the aviation system, on which its success as a company depends. Boeing representatives describe the 9/11 attack consequences on the aviation system as damaging to the company, accounting for staggering losses in anticipated sales.

Boeing has worked closely with TSA and a risk management working group, consisting of government and industry representatives, to specify the threats and vulnerabilities represented in the model; to collect critical input values from TSA subject matter experts; to accurately depict TSA and airport operations, security procedures, and equipment performance; and to define case studies that could be analyzed with RMAT that would benefit TSA decisionmaking.

The first production run of RMAT using classified servers and input data occurred in 2008. Since then, the model and many of its parameters have continued to be developed and refined. Personnel from TSA's Risk Analysis and Capabilities Design (RACD) meet monthly with Boeing RMAT staff, developing countermeasure case studies to understand the risk reductions associated with, for instance, Advanced Imaging Technology (AIT), Explosives Trace Detection Systems (ETDS), behavior detection officers (BDOs), and federal air marshals.

The RMAT program is now roughly 60,000 lines of Visual Basic code, with over 4,000 user-modifiable parameters. The model attempts to describe terrorist preferences, capabilities, operational planning, attacks, likelihoods of attack success, and the consequences of successful attacks in the context of a realistic domestic commercial air transportation system equipped with more than two dozen separate security countermeasures.

Boeing describes RMAT as an agent-based model, in which an adversary refines an attack plan using open source information about the air transportation system and by sending "red agents" on reconnaissance missions through a representative airport. The RMAT airport is configured to include the places, activities, and security systems relevant to air transportation security and found at most U.S. airports, including, for instance, curbside check-in locations, checked baggage–handling systems, passenger checkpoints and associated detection systems, employees, access points, etc. As red agents on reconnaissance missions explore this system, they learn of the existence of security systems and refine estimates of the systems'performance.

The adversary's goal is to maximize expected consequences from a selected attack. It uses reconnaissance to select which among 67 candidate attacks (or weapon-target pairings) offers the most attractive option based on several presumed preferences. The adversary also considers the possibility of mounting multiple "parallel attacks" or independent attacks using identical weapon-target pairs but executed by separate teams of red agents. Parallel attacks can greatly increase the expected consequences of attacks but incur more risk and require more resources.

After selecting the attack type and number of parallel attacks, the adversary develops an attack plan that involves acquiring needed resources from a list of resource types that Boeing considers proprietary. The adversary selects an attack pathway (a route through or around the airport) and might plan a "dry run" to learn more about the security systems that red agents will face when executing the real attack. Finally, the attack is executed with damage from multiple possible outcomes calculated.

Because RMAT is a Monte Carlo simulation, RMAT results can differ each time the model is run, even if input parameters are not changed. Therefore, to provide stable estimates of adversary success rates, the attractiveness of different weapon-target pairings, and the expected losses to the defender, the results of 425 RMAT runs with a single set of input values are typically averaged.

To understand the possible benefits of new security countermeasures (e.g., new instruments, improved processes, or personnel improvements), RMAT results with the new countermeasure are compared to results from a "baseline" RMAT run where inputs are selected to represent air transportation security as it currently exists. Comparing risk measures before and after introduction of the countermeasure provides estimates of the risk reduction if certain assumptions discussed in Chapter Six can be made.

In recent practice, TSA has modified the analysis in two important ways. First, instead of allowing the adversary to select what it believes to be the most attractive attack option, the adversary is forced to attempt each attack type, so that the probability of success and consequences from each attack can be estimated. This modified procedure is appealing in that it provides comparative data on the risks of each key vulnerability, conditional on an attack. Moreover, it makes the analysis more robust by not depending on unreliable estimates of the absolute probability of attacks but therefore gives more weight than it "should" to attacks that are, in fact, quite unlikely. The dilemma on which way to tilt on such matters is a standard problem encountered in policy analytic work of this type and is taken up in greater detail later in this report.

The second important modification is that TSA does not use RMAT estimates of expected defender consequences of attacks, favoring instead estimates of attack consequences generated by another TSA risk-assessment process, the Transportation Sector Security Risk Assessment (TSSRA; TSA, 2010). Thus, TSA calculates independent estimates of expected losses by multiplying RMAT probabilities of success for individual attacks by TSSRA estimates of the likely consequences of those attacks.

Validation of RMAT

RMAT belongs to a growing class of quantitative models that are complex and cannot be directly tested by comparing model predictions to the outcome of events in the real world, because there are too few comparable terrorist attacks against the air transportation system to support statistical inferences about RMAT validity. Such models, like the large force-on-force military campaign models that have been used for decades, now include Department of Defense (DoD) efforts to model diplomatic, information, military, economic, financial, intelligence, and law enforcement responses to U.S. activities (e.g., Phillips, Crosscope, and Geddes, 2008; Body and Marston, 2011); and other terrorism risk models under development at the Department of Homeland Security and the Department of Defense (NRC, 2010; DoD, 2011).

Validation of complex models has been a key concern of the military simulations community for over three decades. Since 1991, the Military Operations Research Society has organized a series of "SIMVAL" workshops on this topic, and other researchers, vendors, and organizations have also tried to clarify what it means for complex simulations to be valid and under what circumstances they can be found to be so (e.g., Davis, 1992; Ritchie, 1992; Hodges and Dewar, 1992; Dewar et al., 1996; Hartley, 1997; Bigelow and Davis, 2003; Pace, 2004; Chaturvedi et al., 2008; Hodges, 1991; Sargent, 2005).

Much of this work has been done by RAND, and so we draw heavily on our own work for this discussion.

DoD Instruction 5000.61 defines model validation as "the process of determining the degree to which a model and its associated data are an accurate representation of the real world from the perspective of the intended use of the model." In other words, a model may be valid for one set of uses but invalid for another. In addition, validity requires not just a model able to accurately describe the world, but input data required by the model must also be accurate. We know how to accurately model an arrow's flight path, for instance, but without input data on its speed and direction when it leaves the bow, our analysis will be invalid for predicting where it might land. If the model or the data it uses are not accurate, its results may be completely wrong, so the uses for which the model can credibly or validly support are narrowed.

There are distinct validity criteria for different classes of uses (Dewar et al., 1996). At a high level of abstraction, we distinguish among three types of uses for simulation models such as RMAT, each requiring different validity criteria. Strongly predictive models are those designed to mirror reality with known precision. Models or analyses used to predict the future on such high-stakes questions as "will the astronauts be safe" or "will the multimillion dollar security program reduce risk" represent a class of uses with the most demanding validity requirements (Dewar et al., 1996). Predictive validity requires that both the model and its data accurately describe reality.

As in the case of complex meteorological models, strongly predictive models need not be consistently accurate, but validation requires understanding the distribution of prediction errors expected for the model (Dewar et al., 1996). Therefore, validation requires a strong basis in settled theory and, ultimately (even if in long-ago experiments), a sufficiently large empirical basis for judging the model's reliability. This is a standard that terrorism risk models cannot hope to achieve.

There is sufficient weather data to compare weather model results to hundreds of historical events with roughly comparable input conditions. The same is not true for terrorism that has as many critically important input factors to consider but a comparative poverty of historical evidence. Even in such cases as air transportation terrorism with reasonably large numbers of historical events (e.g., see Chapter Two), changing security environments, terrorist groups, their objectives, and their tactics results in very few events that share enough similarity to provide a set of test cases for any particular set of model inputs.

A second class of model uses involves understanding phenomena; refining theories and analysis strategies; supporting exploratory modeling (discussed more later); generating new insights; and recording, preserving, and conveying knowledge. When the conceptual models on which these simulations are built are good, these models would be predictive if accurate input data were available. When conceptual foundations are less well developed, these models can support theory development for complex phenomena by promoting rigorous and detailed analysis of what is and is not known about the modeled phenomena.

For instance, consider a model designed to account for how risks might shift to less well-defended targets after introduction of a security countermeasure. The process of designing such a model can trigger important conceptual developments concerning how adversary resources and capabilities affect such shifts, about adversaries' utility functions (What range of objectives might they have? Do they pursue optimizing or satisficing outcomes?), about how imperfect information or predispositional biases might affect target choice, etc. Working through such considerations can result in a new, possibly testable theory of adversary behavior. By identifying important factors that may not have been previously considered, such model development can help to inform analysts, decisionmakers, and the low-resolution models that can be used to rigorously evaluate policy options. Insights from these models can also help identify data requirements that can be used to focus intelligence collection or research efforts. We argue in this report that RMAT is well suited for these uses.

A third class of uses involves informing decisionmaking. These models are specifically designed to address the major factors affecting decisions under consideration and are designed to help decisionmakers understand how important sources of uncertainty affect the likely outcomes of their decisions. That is, these models are designed to support exploratory analysis (Davis, 2002). For instance, by exploring modeled outcomes across the range of possible values on uncertain input variables, it might be possible to establish the conditions under which a new security technology appears to be effective and those under which it does not. In contrast to strongly predictive uses, for which the most likely outcomes are calculated, exploratory analysis can be used to understand the range of possible outcomes given sources of deep uncertainty in either the input data or the conceptual model. Such analyses are particularly valuable for decisionmakers who cannot predict future conditions with accuracy, so wish to select policies that are robust across the range of plausible futures.

Validation of analytic methods for exploratory uses does not necessarily require demonstrating predictive validity. Nevertheless, trusting a model to correctly reveal how key uncertainties could affect outcomes requires a credible conceptual model for which any uncertainties in, for instance, causal relationships can be explored, and where data used as inputs (as opposed to those that are treated as sources of uncertainty) are accurate.

As such, establishing the utility and credibility of analyses used for exploratory analysis requires assessing the credibility of the conceptual models and input data used to support them, and carefully documenting the assumptions, uncertainties, and conjectures on which any predictions rest. Tools using rigorous data and conceptual models can be said to be valid for exploratory analyses. As the credibility of the conceptual models or the data declines, the utility of the model for exploratory analysis suffers a corresponding decline.

Models that are clearly unsuited to exploratory analysis (too many variables, too many uncertainties) often serve other critical functions. We argue in this report that RMAT could be used to contribute to a valuable program of exploratory analysis for decision support at TSA, though RMAT alone is not designed to perform exploratory analyses of the type we describe in Chapter Six.

How, then, do we evaluate RMAT? TSA itself has emphasized that RMAT and the associated risk-management analysis processes (RMAP) for using RMAT results are chiefly useful for gaining insights into the benefits that new or contemplated security programs might offer. Quoting from one TSA document we reviewed (TSA, undated-b):

The overall RMAP can serve to

- inform resource allocation with risk-informed calculations and other cost-benefit information
- provide a structured framework for modeling and evaluating different risk information and perspectives
- inform the design and deployment of countermeasures considering people, processes, and technology in the aviation system.

RMAT could inform policy and resource allocation decisions in many ways, with a corresponding variety of validation requirements. If RMAT is used to estimate the risk reductions likely to be produced by a new screening technology at the checkpoint, a new passenger screening process such as the introduction of the 3-1-1 liquid carry-on requirement, or a new security program such as TSA's Screening Passengers by Observational Technique (SPOT) detection officers, this represents a strongly predictive use, requiring demonstration of RMAT predictive validity. In contrast, where RMAT is used to enrich understanding of terrorism risk and its features, to explore the possible implications of different assumptions, or to drive improvements in conceptual models of terrorism risk, such uses can produce valuable insights without requiring reliable predictive validity.

Throughout this report, we will consider the RMAT validity for each of these uses.

Requirements Development and Validation

In addition to being validated for specific uses, models are validated against specific requirements. That is, we must specify what information the model is designed to produce.

Typically, tools such as RMAT are built to satisfy a set of explicit requirements, and so validation entails establishing that the requirements have been adequately fulfilled. In the case of RMAT, however, no comprehensive requirements document was developed. Originally conceived as a prototype decision support tool, RMAT has evolved into a large-scale system for estimating the risk-reduction benefits of counterterrorism security systems for the U.S. aviation system. As it has evolved, new uses and requirements have emerged.

Without an authoritative set of requirements statement, it is not possible to establish whether RMAT met its intended functionality. Instead, therefore, RAND documented TSA's current intended uses for its risk-assessment processes and its current high-level risk-assessment and analysis requirements, to evaluate which among this broader set of requirements RMAT satisfies. We collected a broad set of intended uses, some of which focus more on the functional requirements of the risk-assessment process and others that concern the uses to which TSA wishes to be able to put resulting risk estimates.

We adapted a standard software engineering approach to compile the requirements for a TSA risk-management analysis tool (Pfleeger and Atlee, 2006). Specifically, we consulted existing documentation regarding RMAT capabilities from TSA, guidance for such tools offered by the Government Accountability Office (GAO, 2009), the National Infrastructure Protection Plan (NIPP; DHS, 2009), and others. Additionally, we conducted interviews with program managers and officials from TSA, stakeholders in the aviation community, and the Boeing Company to solicit requirements.

Because we collected requirements and intended uses for TSA's risk-assessment needs generally, we have no expectation that RMAT should be able to satisfy them all. Instead, we consider in this report which of TSA's current needs can be met with RMAT and which require other tools or methods.

The results of this effort revealed 23 high-level TSA-intended uses and requirements for its terrorism risk assessment (see the appendix for the complete list of intended uses and requirements). We consider each of these requirements in the chapters that follow.

Approach to Validating RMAT

This report describes RAND's efforts to validate RMAT for a set of TSA intended uses. These validation efforts considered diverse sources of evidence, including published scientific literature, elicited subject matter expert judgments, considerations of logic and reasonableness, historical evidence, and quantitative empirical analysis of RMAT and its outputs.

Our efforts were divided across four substantive research questions:

1. Are the adversary behavior and air transportation system conceptual models complete and accurate? We evaluate the adversary conceptual model in Chapter Two and the air transportation system in Chapter Three.

2. Are the data used to inform RMAT parameters valid, and are procedures for collecting, managing, and updating these data sufficient to ensure their continued validity (Chapter Four)?

3. Does the RMAT code, as implemented, perform in the way it was designed to? In Chapter Five, we approach this question using direct inspection of the code and its properties, sensitivity analyses, and independent calculations of expected values.

4. Can risk estimates from RMAT be used in the ways TSA intends (Chapter Six).

Each chapter assesses RMAT in terms of these questions and makes recommendations for further improvements to RMAT and TSA's risk-assessment approach. In Chapter Seven, we summarize our observations and recommendations.

CHAPTER TWO

RMAT Adversary Model

A core feature of RMAT is an adaptive adversary who weighs the advantages of alternative attack strategies, learns new information about the aviation system, and plans and attempts to execute an attack.[1] This chapter assesses the RMAT conceptualization of terrorist adversaries, with the objective of establishing whether it adequately captures the range of capabilities, decisions, and behaviors of potential adversaries. We first provide an overview of the RMAT adversary model and distill key aspects of the model into ten propositions about adversary behavior. The second section assesses the accuracy of the propositions based on their congruence with the social science literature and empirical evidence. The third section assesses whether the adversary model satisfies TSA requirements for adversary modeling.

Overview of the RMAT Adversary Model

The RMAT adversary model is a representation of the essential behavioral and organizational characteristics of a spectrum of terrorist threats to the U.S. aviation system. The purpose of the model is to represent the adversary accurately enough to allow a realistic test and comparison of countermeasures for aviation-focused terrorist attacks. It is designed to simulate aspects of the adversary's behavior and organization that

---

[1] As described later in this section, RMAT can be run in two modes. Currently, it is run in a mode where the weapon and target are predefined. RMAT does have the capability to be run in a competition mode where the adversary selects a weapon and target of choice.

are likely to affect its attack preferences and success rates against a set of countermeasures.

RMAT was not built to implement an established, comprehensive theory of how terrorists behave. Instead, RMAT collects the insights and intuitions of its designers, subject matter experts who have participated in its development, and TSA intelligence analysts and officials who have worked with it over the years. Since there is no authoritative statement of the theory of adversary behavior implemented in RMAT, we have extracted from the model a series of factual propositions about red behavior that are implied by either the model's architecture, the input data currently used by it, or the manner in which RMAT is currently used. We then seek confirming or disconfirming evidence from the social science and other literatures to validate these core model propositions.

The model's representation of the adversary's conduct can be broken down into four categories—organizational characteristics, learning, attack-planning, and behavior. The following sections describe the categories in detail and identify their constituent propositions.

Organizational Characteristics

The adversary's organization can vary on more than a dozen dimensions, and its capabilities can be set to range from incompetence to deadly sophistication.

The model allows the user to define a terrorist group based on 114 variables that describe the adversary's resources, capabilities, tactics, preferences, and objectives. The model, as it is current used, features three classes of terrorist groups, each associated in different ways with al-Qa'ida (AQ) and the global Salafi Jihadist movement, which are specified by a set of parameter values.[2] The most sophisticated of the threats are groups directly linked to the central leadership of al-Qa'ida (Core) and the least sophisticated are local cells of "aspirant" jihadists (Aspirants). In between these extremes are al-Qa'ida associates and franchises (Franchise), which are only loosely connected to the Core.

---

[2] RMAT allows for many adversaries to be created and characterized by different combinations of 114 variables, but it currently features only three adversaries.

Each class differs in sophistication according to its members' years of experience, the geographic scope of its cell "networks" (i.e., local, national, and international), and the extent to which it is logistically connected to the AQ Core. Table 2.1 highlights features of the Core, Franchise, and Aspirant adversary categories and provides the associated RMAT terminology.

Adversaries may differ in terms of their organizational disposition, such as the group's risk tolerance, the characteristics of each phase of the operational cycle (e.g., reconnaissance, attack-planning), resources, and the importance it assigns to each of several operational obstacles it anticipates, such as how long it will take to mount the attack. The adversary's organizational disposition is reflected uniformly in the behavior of the adversary agents.

Learning

The RMAT adversary is a learning organization. Adversary understanding of the strengths and vulnerabilities of the aviation security system evolves over time. The rate of learning depends on a number of factors, such as the skill of adversary agents engaged in a variety of available intelligence collection activities and assumptions about how new information modifies the adversary's beliefs. A learning function establishes the incremental information gained from each mission.

Attack-Planning

The RMAT adversary selects an attack based on its attractiveness, which is determined by multiple adversary preferences and its perception of the expected risks and consequences of the attack. The adversary

Table 2.1
Key Aspects of the Adversary Threat Spectrum

Adversary Name	RMAT Name	Years of Experience	Geographic Range of Network	Connection to AQ Core
Core	High	1–10	International	Yes
Franchise	Hybrid	1–5	National	Limited
Aspirant	Low	1–5	Local	No

calculates the attack's consequences as a combination of the expected direct and indirect economic costs, deaths, and psychological impact. The adversary's estimation of the property damage and indirect economic effects are substantially greater than the defender's estimation of these costs.[3] Because estimates of indirect economic costs used in RMAT dwarf direct costs, adversaries are biased toward attacks with high indirect costs. As the model is currently used, the psychological impact of an attack is not one of the factors considered by the adversary when selecting an attack.[4]

The weights assigned to direct and indirect economic costs, deaths, and psychological impact can be modified but have not been for the case studies we examined. In each case, the dollar values of deaths, direct costs, and indirect costs are summed to produce an attractiveness for each type of attack (see Chapter Three for a discussion of these values). Actual attack attractiveness is reduced by more than a half dozen factors thought to contribute to the adversary's estimate of the risks and benefits likely to result from the attack. After determining attack attractiveness for each attack, including attacks involving multiple parallel attacks, the adversary selects the most attractive one.

The magnitude of several cost inputs can vary depending on the adversary group type. The AQ Core has the highest tolerance for delays and attack complexity and the lowest tolerance for operational risks and expenditures. Aspirant groups have the highest tolerance for operational risks and expenditures and the lowest tolerance for delays and attack complexity. Adversary type also determines some aspects of attack-planning sophistication—specifically, the AQ Core group will plan more sophisticated operations than Aspirants will.

---

[3] The property damage estimates are greater because the adversary assumes a replacement value whereas the defender assumes a depreciated value. The indirect cost estimates are greater to capture the impact of the attack beyond the commercial aviation system and to reflect the adversary's desire to inflict damage on the wider society. This approach to estimating expected consequences is discussed in Chapter Three.

[4] The model is designed to allow monetized estimates of the psychological value of attacks to be incorporated into adversary attractiveness calculations. Because such values are difficult or impossible to estimate, the psychological value of all attacks is currently set at $0. We discuss this issue further in Chapter Six.

The adversary is currently limited to one of 67 available "effects" or types of attack, which include carry-on bombs, checked baggage bombs, cargo bombs, hijackings, insider-assisted attacks, terminal attacks, truck bomb attacks, and stand-off airport attacks. Most types of attacks have separate insider-assisted and noninsider-assisted variations.

Once the adversary settles on the most attractive attack, attack-planning shifts to attack construction. Adversaries attempt the most attractive attack type available to them. Although risk of failure factors into the calculation of attack attractiveness, it is still possible for an attack with a low probability of success to emerge as the most attractive choice. In practice, this means that there is no deterrence and no shifting of attacks to softer targets outside those selected for consideration in any model run. However, an attack that takes more than ten years (in the modeled world) to plot and execute is de facto deterred, as the attack "times out" in the model.[5]

The adversary considers the optimal number of parallel attacks of the same type but does not consider orchestrating multiple, simultaneous attacks using diverse methods. RMAT assumes that with each additional parallel attack, indirect consequences rise almost linearly, up to the maximum number of parallel attacks set by the user. After the maximum is reached, the model assumes that there are no additional indirect consequences associated with additional attacks.

Behavior

Before attacks, adversary behavior consists of random reconnaissance (before a target is selected), directed reconnaissance (after a target is selected), defense-stressing missions,[6] dry run missions, resource acquisition activities, and adversary learning. The adversary can be detected during security screening and interrogation procedures, depending on

---

[5]   By convention, RMAT has been set to run each scenario for ten model years. This time period is an input value that can be changed.

[6]   In RMAT, defense-stressing missions will give additional information to the adversary about the capabilities of blue defenses. It represents the adversary testing the capabilities of blue security measures (e.g., determining how well TSA can identify bomb-like objects hidden in luggage).

both adversary and defender skill levels and other factors, and can vary in reconnaissance skills. Agent detection can trigger interrogation or additional screening; agent reconnaissance skill levels determine how much adversaries can learn about defensive systems.

Attack behavior is manifest in three principal postattack outcomes—full success, partial success, and complete failure. An attack is classified as a full success when all of the attack objectives are accomplished. An attack is a partial success when only a portion of the attack objectives is accomplished—for example, a bomb is detonated during a flight but does not catastrophically disable the aircraft. Complete failure occurs when none of the attack objectives are accomplished.

Assessment of the Implicit Theory of Adversary Behavior and Decisionmaking in RMAT

Assessing a model of this type depends on assessing whether the model behaves in a manner consistent with what we know and what we believe based on evidence or reason. Under ideal circumstances we could validate the adversarial model against an empirical database derived from previous terrorist events and knowledge of their internal workings. Since such a database would be limited at best, we establish the level of credibility of the adversarial model by assessing the soundness of the theory it uses. The RMAT adversary model was not constructed to implement an established theory of adversary behaviors, as there were none that sought to explain terrorist behavior at the high level of detail selected for RMAT. Instead, it implements a set of beliefs, estimates, and assumptions offered by subject matter experts, intelligence analysts, and others who have been involved in the development of RMAT. The resulting theory of adversary behavior has not been fully documented, apart from its instantiation in the model's code and in detailed briefings of some of its component functions. To evaluate the credibility of this implicit theory, we have identified a series of propositions about adversaries, representing factual claims or beliefs that underlie the RMAT adversary model. In the following sections, we describe the implied propositions within RMAT and assess the congruence of each with existing theory and evidence.

Organizational Characteristic Propositions

The spectrum of threats to the U.S. aviation system falls somewhere between the AQ Core, AQ Franchises, and low-skill Aspirants.[7] This range is a practical starting point, but it excludes some potential threats, such as high-skill Aspirants. Aspirants vary widely in sophistication, so characterizing most Aspirants as low-skilled is unrealistic. The Aspirants responsible for the 2004 Madrid train bombings employed their extensive knowledge of the local environment and criminal world to facilitate their attack. Although they were not highly sophisticated, they were clever enough to evade security measures and complete their attack (Kenney, 2010). Aspirants conducted the 2005 London transit bombings, which were relatively sophisticated and well planned (HSI, 2007). This may be important for the model because a high-skill ranking could produce an unexpected multiplying effect when coupled with other aspirant characteristics such as high risk tolerance or their presumed willingness to use more of their resources on attacks.

The primary characteristics distinguishing different adversaries concern their preferences, resources, tactics, skills, and learning, and these differences are specific and quantifiable. RMAT allows for variation in most of the key features that differentiate groups and their capabilities. Assigning values to these parameters is challenging, however. Some Aspirants with no experience in militancy have proven analytically savvy, and some of the experienced AQ Core cells have proven analytically obtuse (Jordan, Mañas, and Horsburgh, 2008). Some groups are better than others at learning from their experiences and deciding whether the information they are using to make decisions is wrong (Jackson, 2009). A group with a high analytic capability would be better at identifying whether its capabilities are matched

---

[7]   Many of these propositions are influenced by the input values currently selected for use by RMAT. RMAT has the flexibility to incorporate different adversaries with custom behaviors. Because RMAT results are only as good as the model and its inputs, we evaluate both here, but note in Table 2.3 (below) whether propositions rest chiefly on data inputs, model architecture, or TSA uses of RMAT results.

or mismatched with a given security and detection regime, which is an important determinant of terrorist operational success and failure (Jackson and Frelinger, 2009).

Adversary Learning Propositions

Adversaries use multiple reconnaissance, dry run, and defense-stressing missions to learn about the aviation security system. Although many adversaries conduct basic, physical reconnaissance, the model's current data inputs likely overestimate the volume of these targeted reconnaissance missions per plot. Highly productive information-gathering activities, such as dry run and defense-stressing missions, are extremely rare. Although current data inputs for the number of such physical reconnaissance missions are too high, reconnaissance, dry run, and defense-stressing missions can be adjusted in RMAT. RMAT also accounts for "virtual" reconnaissance—intelligence collected on the Internet, for example, which is very likely to be a common practice among terrorist groups.

Known examples of physical reconnaissance involve only very basic data collection (e.g., driving around the perimeter of an airport, passing through security checkpoints without "testing" the security procedures, or making routine observations about the defender's methods for searching personal bags). As law enforcement efforts have increasingly targeted terrorist plotting, the actual and perceived likelihood of being caught conducting surveillance and reconnaissance missions has grown (Kenney, 2010). This may explain the low incidence of productive or probing missions. Table 2.2 provides details on a selection of aviation attacks and plots directed at U.S. and United Kingdom (U.K.) targets since 1995 and the observed incidence of terrorist reconnaissance and dry run missions.[8] For the majority of these cases, when reconnaissance was conducted it was limited and basic, as noted in the table. Additionally, reconnaissance missions can be expensive (e.g., the

---

[8] Information is approximate and based on U.S. court documents, official accounts, and media accounts. The data do not include dry runs or reconnaissance missions that were not detected by intelligence or law enforcement authorities. The selection of attacks is considered quasirandom because these are plots for which information was available in open sources.

Table 2.2
A Selection of Aviation Attacks and Plots Directed at U.S. or U.K. Targets and the Prevalence of Reconnaissance, Dry Runs, and Insider Assistance

Plot	Date	Group	Successful Attack	Reconnaissance/ Surveillance	Dry Runs	Insider Assistance
Arif Uka—Germany shooting	2011	Aspirant	Yes	Probably limited	No	Yes
Cargo bomb plot	2010	AQAP	No	No	Possibly	No
Rajib Karim—British Airways employee	2010	AQAP	No	Yes	No	Yes
Christmas Day plot	2009	AQAP	No	Unknown	No	No
Air National Guard plot	2009	Aspirant	No	Limited	No	No
Glasgow Airport attack	2008	Aspirant	No	Probably limited	No	No
JFK Airport plot	2007	Aspirant	No	Limited	No	Yes
Transatlantic plot	2006	Aspirant/ Core	No	Unknown	Possibly planned	No
LAX Airport—El Al ticket counter shooting	2002	Other	Yes	Unknown	No	No
Shoe-bomber	2001	Hybrid	No	Limited	Unknown	No
9/11	2001	AQ Core	Yes	Yes	Yes	No
Millennium plot—LAX Airport	1999	AQ Core	No	Probably limited	No	No
Bojinka plot	1995	AQ Core	No	Yes	Yes	No

NOTE: AQAP is Al-Qa'ida in the Arabian Peninsula.

cost of multiple first-class airline tickets) and, as a result, less attractive than publicly available information, which is relatively inexpensive. It stands to reason that cost sensitivity probably affects Aspirant groups' decisionmaking more than that of less financially strapped Core and Franchise plotters.

Attack-Planning Propositions

The adversary selects an attack based on its attractiveness. The literature mostly supports the notion that terrorist groups select targets and devise attack strategies in a calculated, rational manner (Morral and Jackson, 2009).

AQ Core has the highest tolerance for delays and attack complexity and the lowest tolerance for operational risks and expenditures. Aspirant groups have the highest tolerance for operational risks and expenditures and the lowest tolerance for delays and attack complexity. That AQ Core groups have the lowest tolerance for risk is partially contradicted by the literature and by well-known facts (does anyone imagine that the 9/11 attack was low risk?). According to a study by the Combating Terrorism Center, plots tied to AQ senior leaders were successful only 50 percent of the time, whereas plots produced by the movement (Aspirants) were much more likely to succeed (Helfstein and Wright, 2011). According to the study, the Core is likely taking bigger risks for a bigger payoff, usually against more symbolic and hardened targets. This produces more disrupted plots but more casualties overall and possibly a greater psychological impact. One interpretation of these data is that some Aspirants chose softer targets to maximize their success given limited resources and training, which may indicate that Aspirants have a lower tolerance for risk.

The second element of the proposition—that AQ Core groups have the highest tolerance for delays—is neither strongly supported nor contradicted by the literature. The AQ Core's patience with the planning of 9/11 appears to be consistent with this proposition, but even this attack was shaped by time considerations—Osama bin Ladin was alleged to have rejected an additional attack against a nuclear reactor because "there was not enough time to prepare for an operation" (Lichtblau, 2003). Some Core plots, such as the Millennium attempt, suffered from apparent impatience and hasty preparation. Some Aspirant plots, in contrast, such as the London transit bombings, experienced setbacks and delays that likely tested the group's patience but were executed successfully nonetheless.

The third element of this proposition seems to be mostly correct. Aspirant groups tend to be small and resource-constrained, leaving them less likely to plan or execute complex attacks. There are several examples, however, of Aspirants conducting successful complex attacks (e.g., the 2005 London transit bombings).

Finally, RMAT correctly assumes that as attack complexity increases, so too does the risk of discovery and failure (Enders and Su, 2007; Helfstein and Wright, 2011). One reason for this is that complex attacks require more attackers with more skills, additional technology (e.g., communications), and additional interactions among members (Jackson and Frelinger, 2009).

Adversaries attempt the most attractive attack type available to them, no matter how low they perceive their chances of success to be. RMAT correctly assumes that as the probability of success decreases, the attractiveness of an attack decreases. Nevertheless, adversaries are obliged in RMAT to mount an attack, even if none of the attack options stands a good chance of success. In practice, this means that there is no deterrence and no shifting of attacks to softer targets outside those selected for consideration in any model run, such as targets outside the aviation system.[9] The principal limitation with this proposition is that many terrorist groups are keenly and explicitly averse to undertaking operations that appear to have a poor chance of success, and, in reality, attackers always have the option of shifting their attack to an easier target (Morral and Jackson, 2009). Some groups are better than others at estimating their chances of success and adjusting their plotting accordingly, likely producing some variation between groups in the ability to shift strategies (Jackson, 2009).

---

[9] TSA recognizes that deterrence is not well handled in RMAT and has developed a "threat-shifting methodology" it uses in interpreting findings from RMAT and other analyses. We did not assess the TSA threat-shifting methodology.

In competition mode (i.e., where the adversary selects an attack from among a set of options), this proposition can exhibit risk-shifting within the aviation system in ways supported by social science theory. Enders and Sandler (1993) argue that policy measures that made certain terrorist modes of attack more difficult resulted in terrorists immediately substituting into other attack modes. For example, ground-based aviation attacks (e.g., vehicle bombs outside airports and bombs inside airports) have recently become relatively more common than attacks inside airplanes (Jackson and Frelinger, 2012; Berrebi, 2009). Jackson and Frelinger surmise that ground attacks are simpler and less logistically demanding. Brandt and Sandler (2010) argue that as governments succeeded in stopping terrorist operations, some terrorists shifted their focus to harder-to-defend targets. Shughart (2006) notes that terrorist hijackings of commercial aircraft declined in favor of other hostage-taking missions after airport security was tightened by installing metal detectors to screen passengers.

The attack's consequences are a combination of the maximum possible direct and indirect economic costs, deaths, one-time government costs (such as purchasing new security technology to prevent repeats of any successful attack), and psychological impacts, and the values assigned to these factors are relatively constant across adversaries. This proposition has a number of limitations. First, the values assigned to different outcomes will vary both within and between terrorist groups. Even within the subset of terrorist operations against aviation targets, operational objectives have varied widely—some were designed to produce disruption and others focused on destruction (Jackson and Frelinger, 2012). Drake argues that ideological differences between terrorist groups produce differences in the targeting patterns, even between groups that have superficially similar but distinct ideologies (Drake, 1998).

An objective that is not contemplated in this proposition is that attacks may be designed to influence the adversary's own constituents and sympathizers, an objective that may or may not directly relate to the ideological agenda the group pursues (Crenshaw, 2001). This component would include the attack's estimated effect on the group's morale, prestige, and recruitment rates. Leading jihadi strategist Mustafa Setmariam commented that the criteria for targets should be selected based on (1) where it hurts the enemy the most and (2) where it awakens Muslims and revives the spirit of jihad and resistance (Cruickshank and Ali, 2007). A terrorist group's target selection may reflect their desire to produce this type of beneficial psychological impact.

RMAT includes a parameter that allows for the idiosyncratic preferences a group's leader may hold that pushes a group toward irrational preoccupations with certain kinds of attack (e.g., the Aum Shinrikyo leader's fixation with poisons) (Jackson, 2009). However, as such characteristics are highly specific to individual groups, data are not available to properly set this variable for most cases to date.

The estimated psychological impact of an attack does not affect the adversary's calculation of an attack's attractiveness. RMAT includes a parameter meant to describe the monetized value of the psychological consequences of different attack types. To date, this parameter has been zeroed out of analyses not because psychological consequences are unimportant but because the problem of estimating and monetizing these effects has not been solved. Notwithstanding these estimation difficulties, this proposition is almost certainly incorrect.

A terrorist group's estimate of the psychological impact of its attack often plays a large role in its decisionmaking and target selection. Libicki, Chalk, and Sisson (2007) found that most al-Qa'ida attacks have been designed to coerce a targeted population—which is largely a psychological objective—in part by threatening future attacks of the same kind. Indeed, most observers would agree that psychological effects like persuading a country to change its foreign policy represent one of the principal objectives of terrorism. Most al-Qa'ida attacks, for instance, have been designed to coerce a targeted population, rather than simply induce short- or long-term economic costs (Libicki, Chalk, and Sisson, 2007). Al-Qa'ida's long-held goal of forcing the withdrawal of U.S. military forces from Muslim countries is a clear example of the group's interest in leveraging the psychological impact of their attacks to change U.S. foreign policy goals in ways that cannot be readily monetized.

Relatedly, one-time government costs (such as purchasing new security technology following a successful attack) have also been set to zero in the model, presumably because there is no consensus on what the correct value would be. It seems unlikely, however, that terrorist groups would give little or no consideration to the estimated cost of the government's security adaptations when they select a target.[10]

Because psychological effects and one-time government costs represent prominent effects in Core and Franchise adversaries, and possibly others, the omission of these factors represents a key shortcoming of the existing model. These omissions reflect the unavailability of valid data that could be used to specify these parameters. To the extent that the model has been designed to require monetization of constructs that may not best be represented with a single monetary dimension, these may also be viewed as limitations of the model's design.

Adversary Behavior Propositions

The adversary's preattack behavior consists of random reconnaissance (before a target is selected), directed reconnaissance (after a target is selected), defense-stressing missions, dry run missions, resource acquisition activities, and adversary learning. As noted above, most known reconnaissance missions were rudimentary and quite limited in number. If a dry run is defined as running through a large part of an operation without actually conducting the attack, then few plots in the sample set of 13 involved dry runs (see Table 2.2). The Bojinka plot, the 9/11 attacks, and the AQAP cargo bombing plot included some active testing of security regimes, but many other plots do not appear to include such behavior. We believe that the current settings used with RMAT that call for multiple physical reconnaissance missions likely overstate the level of reconnaissance that should be expected from most adversaries.

Summary of Select Propositions

The following table summarizes our assessment of the validity of the propositions discussed above. Some of these propositions concern how the model is constructed, some concern the data inputs used to set parameter values, and some concern how TSA uses the model. We

---

[10] This is another case where RMAT has the flexibility in a parameter value that is difficult to establish. Also, as reported in *Inspire*, an online jihadi magazine, one-time government costs to western governments was a major objective of the printer bomb attack.

have distinguished each of these in Table 2.3 as propositions that concern features of the model's "architecture" or "inputs." For those prop-

Table 2.3
Evaluation of Select RMAT Adversary Propositions

Model Proposition	Evidence	Type
The spectrum of threats to the U.S. aviation system falls somewhere between the AQ Core, AQ Franchises, and low-skill Aspirants.	Uncertain	Input
The primary characteristics distinguishing different adversaries concern their preferences, resources, tactics, skills, and learning, and these differences are specific and quantifiable.	Uncertain	Architecture and inputs
Adversaries use multiple reconnaissance, dry run, and defense-stressing missions to learn the aviation security system.	Uncertain	Input
The adversary selects an attack based on its attractiveness.	Strong	Architecture
The AQ Core has the highest tolerance for delays and attack complexity and the lowest tolerance for operational risks and expenditures. Aspirant groups have the highest tolerance for operational risks and expenditures and the lowest tolerance for delays and complexity.	Uncertain	Input
Adversaries attempt the most attractive attack type available to them, no matter how low they perceive their chances of success to be.	Weak	Architecture
The attack's consequences are a combination of the maximum possible direct and indirect economic costs, deaths, one-time government costs (such as purchasing new security technology to prevent repeats of any successful attack), and psychological impacts, and the values assigned to these factors are relatively constant across adversaries.	Weak	Architecture
The estimated psychological impact of an attack does not affect the adversary's calculation of attack attractiveness.	Weak	Architecture and input
The adversary's preattack behavior consists of random reconnaissance (before a target is selected), directed reconnaissance (after a target is selected), defense-stressing missions, dry run missions, resource acquisition activities, and adversary learning.	Uncertain	Architecture and input

ositions with substantial social science or empirical support, we rate the proposition as having a "strong" evidence base. Where evidence is sparse or the proposition receives some confirming and some disconfirming support, we rate it "uncertain." Where we find little evidence of support or evidence contradicting the proposition, we rate it "weak."

Adversary Model: Satisfaction of TSA Requirements

Several of the risk-assessment intended uses and requirements elicited by RAND concerned how adversaries should be conceptualized or modeled. Table 2.4 summarizes our assessments of RMAT performance on two high-priority requirements and one medium-priority adversary requirement.[11]

The medium-priority requirement (6) is to ensure that risk assessments clarify the attack preferences of potential adversaries. RMAT clearly offers such an output.

The first high-priority requirement (Requirement 8) is to depict adversaries that are adaptive and change their actions to evade imple-

Table 2.4
RMAT Adversary Model Satisfaction of Associated TSA Requirements

Requirement	Short Description	RMAT Satisfaction of Requirement
6	Risk assessments should clarify the attack preferences of potential adversaries.	Yes
8	Risk analyses should conceptualize adversaries as adaptive, assessing how risks to the air transportation system change as adversaries attempt to evade countermeasures.	Yes
9	Risk analyses should represent the behavior of all potential adversaries (foreign and domestic; high- and low-skilled) using empirical evidence on such adversaries' behavior and capabilities.	Partially

---

[11] In this table and throughout this report, we provide summary descriptions of the TSA risk-assessment requirements we collected. For more thorough descriptions, see the appendix.

mented countermeasures. RMAT adversaries are designed to be adaptive in several ways. The adversary learns about countermeasures through reconnaissance, and then plans attacks that optimize consequences. Introduction of a countermeasure, therefore, can cause different attacks to be adaptively selected. This adaptiveness is somewhat limited by the model's requirement that adversaries mount some attack, even if none of those available offer much hope of success. The amount of adaptiveness depends in part on what the adversary can learn through reconnaissance. We do not believe there is available information to validate the learning capability of the adversary. Learning is more differentiated by the skill levels assumed for adversaries of different types, as more skilled adversaries are assumed to be able to conduct more productive reconnaissance. As noted above, there is little evidence that terrorists engage in the frequent and productive defense-stressing and dry run missions currently attributed to these more skilled adversaries. Despite these limitations, we judge RMAT to reasonably satisfy Requirement 8.

The second high-priority requirement (9) is to depict adversary behavior that is based on the best empirical evidence or widely accepted estimates of adversary behavior. Although much of the RMAT adversary model is supported by available social science, there are important exceptions. For organizational characteristics, current inputs defining adversary types may not describe an adequate range of adversary planning sophistication, adaptability, or capabilities. Adversary learning propositions almost certainly overemphasize the role of physical reconnaissance, defense-stressing, and dry run missions. Finally, model assumptions about attack planning are not well supported on some issues, including on the variation between adversary types on risk tolerance and the importance of psychological impacts on target selection.

One aspect of this requirement is the importance of modeling adversaries with a range of skill levels. The model does capture such a range with its three types of adversaries (AQ Core, Franchise, and Aspirants), which vary in their levels of sophistication. As the model is currently used, however, some adversary types may not be well represented by these three types, including more capable aspirants.

Recommendations

Here, we recommend a number of improvements that should be considered for the adversary model.

TSA should explore strategies for understanding and conveying the effects of many uncertain parameters in RMAT. Table 2.3 illustrates a fundamental challenge posed by RMAT: how to produce meaningful results for decisionmakers when many of the input data and underlying causal mechanisms are unknown or even unknowable. Currently, RMAT provides the user great flexibility in setting input variables that can capture a wide spectrum of plausible adversary behavior. Flexibility alone is not sufficient when values for these inputs are uncertain. In Chapter Six, we recommended explicitly accounting for uncertainties at a lower level of model resolution so that the range of plausible risk reductions associated with new technologies can be explored to identify robust security strategies.

Attacks with a low probability of success should be modeled as deterred or shifted to softer targets inside or outside the aviation system. Instead of requiring that the adversary attempt to mount one of the attacks made available to it in RMAT, no matter how low he views his chances of success, a more realistic approach might be to include one addition attack option, called "some other attack," with a fixed attractiveness set at a level corresponding to what users believe to be the minimum attractiveness or probability of success that attackers require to proceed with an operation. When other options become less attractive than "some other attack," the suite of available attacks considered in RMAT could be considered to have been deterred, though risk to the aviation system would be reduced only if the possibility of a novel attack against it was ruled out.

Adversaries should exhibit fewer instances of high-risk, high-payoff dry runs and defense-stressing missions. The modeling of these missions probably overestimates what the adversary can learn about the aviation system with active surveillance and overestimates the exposure the adversary has to blue agents in the course of surveillance. This recommendation provides additional realism to what we would expect, but the flexibility of RMAT will allow examination of the effects of terrorists who have better understanding of blue vulnerabilities through multiple dry runs. This gives RMAT the capability to examine rare, catastrophic attacks. This added capability requires the proper, even more stringent, controls with how RMAT is used and how results are interpreted to prevent misinterpretation of results.

The model should account for the adversary's estimation of the psychological impact, impact on its supporters, and one-time government costs of each attack in its calculation of attack attractiveness. The model is designed to allow users to input a monetized estimate of the psychological impact of attacks. Difficulty in estimating these values has caused TSA and Boeing to set this parameter to zero, meaning that psychological impacts are not factored into the adversary's decisions. Because we have good reason to believe that many terrorists do consider psychological impacts to be a central objective of their target selection, the current RMAT configuration raises important doubts about the credibility of modeled target selection. It may be that it is not possible to account for all psychological impacts on a single monetized dimension. Accounting for the adversary's interest in the coercive benefits of an attack—for example, by taking an unexpectedly greater risk to orchestrate a radiological attack that induces few economic costs but exacts a large psychological toll—may enhance the accuracy of the model's target-selection output. Creating a new variable that captures the value of noneconomic psychological costs may help to accomplish this task. The variable would play into the calculation of attack attractiveness by assigning a "psychological impact" coefficient to each weapon-target pair. For example, in-flight, chemical, biological, radiological, insider, or parallel attacks might receive a higher psychological impact score than simple, inexpensive, and non–in-flight attacks. The scale might be imprecise, or merely ordinal, but would help to rank attacks based on their relatively psychological impact attractiveness. Because such a scale would be estimated with considerable imprecision, it would need to be considered in the overall RMAT modeling strategy for accounting for the effects of deep uncertainties on model outcomes described in the first recommendation, above.

The spectrum of threats faced by the U.S. air transportation system would be better represented by adding two types of adversaries. Our review of open source literature on aviation threats revealed at least two adversaries that should be added in RMAT analyses. These are a low-skilled, risk-seeking Core group and a high-skilled, risk-averse Aspirant group.

The RMAT adversary model structure and inputs should be determined, along with their uncertainties, from a wider range of sources. Currently, the RMAT structure and inputs for the adversary model have been heavily dependent on TSA intelligence experts. This dependence has been mainly due to the absence of an adversary behavior theory. In our efforts to assess the RMAT adversary model propositions, we found several other resources that should be considered in constructing the adversarial model architecture and determining the proper inputs. Such sources include the terrorism and social science literatures, U.S. court documents, official accounts, media accounts, counterterrorism analyses from the Federal Bureau of Investigation, experts from the broader intelligence community, as well as TSA intelligence experts. Whereas the current model benefits from each such source, more effort is needed to ensure that the best available evidence is used in the model.

CHAPTER THREE

RMAT Defender Model

Overview

Model Scope and the RMAT World

RMAT represents terrorism defense in the aviation system in the context of a virtual "world" that matches the aviation system. The world is the operating space for RMAT—all adversary and defender operations occur as agents (people) and weapons move through the world. The RMAT world includes a comprehensive representation of points at which defender and adversary agents and weapons might pass, such as the curbside, checked baggage inspection, passenger screening points, lobbies, airplanes, freight-processing facilities, and catering kitchens. The RMAT world is an abstraction of the U.S. commercial aviation system. The model focuses on standard operating procedures and equipment that are common to all airports. In so doing, it treats all duplicated elements of the aviation system (e.g., passenger-screening checkpoints) as structurally and functionally identical to each other.[1] Some implications of this choice are discussed below.

The intended scope of RMAT is the U.S. commercial aviation system. This includes the approximately 450 U.S. commercial airports regulated by TSA and all flights departing from or arriving at these airports. While seemingly clear, the boundary to this system is not always obvious. Interfaces with non-U.S. airports, off-airport freight processing, catering, general aviation, mass transit, air traffic control and

---

[1] The RMAT world accounts for differences between large and small airports in how checked baggage is screened.

other information systems, and other off-airport operations can impact U.S. commercial aviation system security. The extent to which RMAT accounts for these interfaces is discussed in subsequent sections.

The defender system in RMAT consists of a variety of different types of blue agents (people) and instruments populating the world, as well as rules describing the conditions under which people may move to different parts of the world.

Blue Agents

The RMAT world is populated by a number of different types of blue agents that have some role in security. These agents include those with security role (e.g., TSA officers, law enforcement officers, federal air marshals) as well as a wide range of agents not nominally focused on security but who may observe suspicious behavior, detect weapons, or perform some other security function (e.g., ticket agents, maintenance workers, freight receivers). Each blue agent type is characterized by a number of attributes. Attribute values are drawn from a distribution for each Monte Carlo run, and all agents of a particular type have the same value for each attribute in an individual Monte Carlo run.

Blue agents occupy space and move within the world. The fraction of time an agent is present in any world location is modeled. Some blue agents are not easily recognizable as blue agents (e.g., undercover airport agents).

Blue agent behavior includes a variety of different actions, such as screening passengers and luggage, resolving detection instrument alarms, observing suspicious activity, and interrogating or apprehending red agents. The actions performed by a given blue agent type are dictated by standard operating procedures.

Instruments

The RMAT world contains instruments. Instruments are classified as either material detectors (e.g., canine or metal detectors) or perception enhancers (e.g., whole-body imagers, video cameras). Instruments are characterized by technical attributes, such as their performance detecting particular quantities of materials used in weapons. Blue agents use instruments and other methods to detect dangerous materials or suspicious activity.

Credentials

Eleven different credentials may be required to move within parts of the world. These credentials are generally either a boarding pass for passengers or a particular type of security identification for employees. Red agents may acquire credentials over the course of a simulation.

Action Outcomes and Decision Points

The outcomes of defender actions in RMAT are determined by functions that depend on attribute values of modeled objects (blue agents, red agents, instruments, weapons) and occasionally other factors. For defender actions, RMAT defines functions for detection by instruments, detection by hand-searching, noticing suspicious activity or bags, and determining outcomes of interrogations. These functions represent one of the key pillars of the RMAT model. They determine the extent to which different combinations of weapons, targets, agent characteristics, and attack pathways will lead to successful attacks. Consequently, model outcomes depend strongly on data and assumptions that make up these functions. The relevant parameters to include in a function, the functional forms, and the parameter value ranges considered are informed by expert input and empirical data. Because of the heavy reliance on data, the case studies include substantial data acquisition efforts.

Function outputs can change over the course of a simulation as a result of adversary actions or learning. Although the attribute values of blue agents, instruments, and weapons are fixed, red agent attribute values and weapon choices can vary among agents and change over the course of a single simulation run as adversary missions progress.

The model also includes several decision points at which a path or action is governed by a probability that is independent of modeled object attributes. These include the probability that an item will be subjected to a particular screening method among multiple allowed methods (e.g., whole body imager versus walk-through metal detector for people, X-ray versus advanced technology X-ray for carry-on luggage,

X-ray versus shoe scanner for shoes, internal versus external explosives trace detection for checked luggage at small airports, multiple screening methods for freight), probabilities that passengers undergo secondary screening at checkpoints and gate areas, and the probability that freight will be loaded onto a freight versus a passenger aircraft.

Validation

Our validation of the defender model in RMAT addressed four areas:

- identifying and evaluating the validity of key assumptions implicit in the overall system design
- comparing the world representation in RMAT to external sources
- assessing the completeness of the attack scenarios considered in RMAT, including both weapon-target pairings and pathways by which attacks are carried out
- comparing the attack consequences modeled in RMAT to external sources.

We validated the defender model primarily against a general criterion that the model be able to estimate reductions in terrorism risk to the commercial aviation system associated with different security tactics. We also discuss the extent to which the defender model addresses those requirements in the appendix that concern RMAT representation of security, air transportation systems, their vulnerabilities, and the consequences of attacks.

Our validation compared assumptions in RMAT to airport design guides, aviation security literature, security policies documented by TSA, and expert input from aviation security practitioners. Subject matter experts were met in-person and provided with an overview of RMAT; a detailed description of the RMAT world, including assumptions about agents, instruments, and credentials; a description of the weapon-target pairings and attack pathways modeled in RMAT; and a list of additional weapon-target pairings and attack pathways not included in RMAT. Experts were asked about the accuracy and completeness of each of these aspects of the defender model. We met with four subject matter experts:

- Shannon Garcia-Hamilton, Federal Security Director, Ontario Airport, CA (TSA, top security person on site, has security approval and oversight responsibility)
- Danny Turner, Assistant Federal Security Director for Law Enforcement, Ontario Airport, CA
- Greg Staar, Commander of Airport Police, Ontario Airport, Ca. (operational responsibility for much of the security)
- Erroll Southers, former Assistant Chief for Homeland Security, Los Angeles Airport Police Department

Additional input and guidance were provided by Randy Harrison from Delta Airlines, Chris Bidwell and Lydia Ortiz from Airports Council International, and Dr. Julie Kim at RAND.

Overall, our validation indicated that the defender system representation in RMAT is a particular strength of the model. However, the model has some gaps that TSA and Boeing should consider remedying, as they could have substantive effects on RMAT results. We also identified several minor errors and omissions. In each case, we briefly summarize the potential impact on the operation and results of RMAT.

Key Assumptions in the RMAT Defender System

There are several general assumptions implicit in the way the defender system in RMAT is represented. We discuss the important assumptions and their implications for the validity of the model.

Defender System Is Static

One general assumption is that the defender system acts only in response to adversary actions. Blue agents respond to red agent actions, and instruments respond to weapons being introduced. The model does not allow for proactive steps during a model run, such as introducing new technology, changing agent assignments, or changing the world. We find that this is a reasonable and, in some sense, necessary assumption given the objectives of RMAT. It is reasonable because, in the course of normal aviation security operations, defender activities are triggered by potential adversary actions. In the longer term, the defender world does, of course, change as new technology and approaches are introduced. However, these are exactly the sorts of changes that RMAT has been developed to evaluate. Thus, the defender system is held constant in an individual RMAT simulation run to provide a baseline for comparison. Changes to the defender system can be implemented by the user in subsequent runs to compare the relative outcomes of the two defender system arrangements.

Use of a Single Abstraction of the Aviation System

Another general assumption is that security risks to and defense of the aviation system can be adequately modeled with a single abstraction of the aviation security system. This assumption has potentially important implications. One is that RMAT cannot model the security idiosyncrasies of individual airports. Security can differ among airports because of design differences (e.g., some have a single, "mega-"passenger screening checkpoint, whereas others have individual passenger screening checkpoints for each terminal or airline). However, airport security is subject to TSA regulation and all must adhere to standard procedure, staffing, and instrumentation requirements (TSA, undated-d). This regulation extends beyond TSA employees to include the roles of local law enforcement and private security staff. Consequently, we have not identified any differences in the inherent design or operation of security that we believe significantly affect the ability of RMAT to assess the value of particular security measures.

Security can also differ among airports because of partial or incomplete deployment of security measures. For example, AIT and BDOs are currently only deployed at a subset of TSA-regulated airports (GAO, 2010a; GAO, 2010b). This is an important consideration because adversaries' risk perceptions may vary across airports depending on the security systems they believe have been implemented, and so they may actively seek out those airports they believe to be more vulnerable. RMAT allows the user to define the probability that an adversary will encounter any security measure, and this functionality can be used to account for partial deployment. In the case of nonvisible security measures, such as BDOs, adversaries cannot selectively avoid them. If BDOs are deployed to airports in a nonpredictable way (i.e., they are not deployed only to the largest airports), then the probability of adversaries' encountering BDOs is equal to the BDO nationwide deployment level. For security measures visible to adversaries, such as AIT, adversaries could deliberately choose locations without AIT. In this case, partial deployment is functionally equivalent to the measure not existing. Alternatively, a less sophisticated adversary may not be able to selectively avoid the technology, in which case the probability of encountering it is equal to its nationwide deployment level. The degree to which an adversary may be willing and able to avoid a partially deployed security measure will depend on the details of the particular measure, so the option to leave this as a user choice in RMAT appears reasonable.

Another implication of using a single abstraction of the U.S. aviation system is that RMAT does not distinguish between security for flights originating within the United States and those originating in another country. Although RMAT is intended to simulate only the domestic commercial aviation system, one important access route to the domestic commercial aviation system is international flights entering the United States. Consequently, security associated with U.S.-bound international flights could be an important addition to RMAT scope. Given that many terrorist threats to U.S. aviation in the past decade derived from inbound international flights (shoe bomber, underwear bomber, and the AQAP printer bombs), the current configuration in RMAT of not modeling differences in security requirements between domestic and international flights represents a shortcoming if these differences are significant.

Our investigation suggests that these differences can indeed be significant. It is difficult to characterize the differences precisely, because the actual security requirements for domestic and international flights are quite general. Practical differences arise in how the requirements are implemented and enforced. TSA has direct control over domestic security activities. In contrast, TSA can influence security on international flights only indirectly, primarily by granting or withholding permission to land in the United States. International airports must conform to some international standards, and TSA has the right to set threshold standards on the security protocols for flights that are bound for U.S. destinations (Electronic Code of Federal Regulations, undated). There are universal standards for such things as liquids. In 2006, more than 70 countries joined an agreement limiting the quantity of liquids passengers are allowed to carry onto a passenger plane (TSA, undated-e). On other issues, there is less standardization. For instance, in the United States, all passengers must remove their shoes (TSA, undated-e), but in Japan, only those wearing "thick-soled" shoes are required to remove them (Japan Airlines, undated).

In addition to variations in how security is implemented, an investigation by the GAO (2011) found that compliance is highly uneven. It found that "some foreign airports complied with all of TSA's aviation security assessment standards; however, TSA has identified serious noncompliance issues at a number of foreign airports. Common areas of noncompliance included weaknesses in airport access controls and passenger and baggage screening." Input from security experts in our study confirms this concern. They noted that differences in security practices exist from country to country and that security practices for many U.S.-bound international flights are not as rigorous as in domestic airports.

The fact that RMAT does not capture these differences is a serious gap that limits its value in assessing the benefit of candidate security improvements. This gap violates Requirement 10, which specifies that "the scope of air transportation risk assessments should be the U.S. commercial aviation system. . . . At a minimum, this should include any vulnerabilities at domestic airports associated with incoming international air cargo and passengers. . . ." Although ambiguities and inconsistencies in security practices among different countries make it difficult to estimate the magnitude of this shortcoming, the fact that so much of the known aviation security risk in the United States is from international flights indicates that the security of international flights must be accurately modeled in RMAT. This gap was previously identified by TSA and Boeing, and efforts are under way to extend RMAT to include international air travel.

Credentials Are Always Required

A third general assumption in the defender system design is that valid credentials are required to move within the world. Consistent with this assumption, RMAT does not include any attack pathways in which red agents attempt to enter world locations without the proper credentials.

In reality, expert feedback on credential validation procedures, along with recent revelations about the frequency of unauthorized entries into restricted areas, suggest that credentials are not always necessary to enter some critical areas. Security experts noted that the air operations area (AOA) boundary on an airfield is typically just a line painted on the pavement and is often unmonitored. This provides relatively easy access to the AOA from adjacent airfield areas, such as freight-processing facilities or general aviation areas. In addition, Stoller (2011) reports that a DHS review found that there have been 14,000 documented cases of unauthorized access to "limited access" areas of U.S. airports, including nearly 5,000 unauthorized entries to the sterile area, or AOA, since 2001. In not modeling the ability to access areas without credentials, RMAT is not capturing some feasible attack pathways that exist in the real world. This also fails to satisfy part of Requirement 11, which specifies that risk assessments should account for "unauthorized access to secure airport areas." We return to this point in the "Pathways" section below.

Blue Agent Skill Levels Are Uniform

A final general assumption about the defender model in RMAT that warrants comment is that all individual blue agents of a particular agent type have the same skill level in any individual Monte Carlo run. This means, for example, that all transportation security officers (TSOs), whether operating metal detectors, X-ray machines, or conducting any other TSO activity, are represented as having the same skill level. Agent skill level is an important parameter in many of the detection probability functions, and allowing it to vary could influence RMAT results. In a simple two-layer security system in which the probability of detection is a constant linear function of agent skill level (i.e., probability = k*skill), it can be shown that the net probability of detection through the two layers when agent skill levels are uniform is always less than that when the average skill level across agents is unchanged but skill levels among individual agents is allowed to vary.[2] Under such conditions, the assumption of uniform skill level would systematically bias the probabilities of detection lower, leading to an underestimate of the actual effectiveness of the defender system. Note that the skill level for each agent type is drawn from a distribution in each Monte Carlo run. So the average skill level in an RMAT simulation consisting of a large number of Monte Carlo runs does reflect a range. The concern with using uniform skill levels in each Monte Carlo run is that detection probabilities in each run may be slightly low, leading to lower detection probabilities overall. Since this value cannot be varied in the current model configuration, it is difficult to assess the magnitude of this effect.

In practice, layers are not identical to each other, and the relationship between detection probability and agent skill level for different layers is not necessarily constant. Consequently, the effect of varying skill levels among agents depends on the details of the relationships and may lead to an underestimation of detection probabilities. Nonetheless, it is clear that varying agent skill level does influence detection probabilities whenever multiple layers act on a single person or object. In neglecting this variation, RMAT may be misrepresenting risks.

World Analysis

We validated the RMAT representation of the aviation system. We also considered whether relevant aviation system characteristics are not

---

[2]   If P_1 is the probability of detection at layer 1 and P_2 is the probability of detection at layer 2, then the total probability of detection through both layers, $P_T = 1 - (1 - P_1)(1 - P_2) = 1 - 1 + P_2 + P_1 - P_1{}^*P_2 = P_1 + P_2(1 - P_1)$. If $P = kS$, where S is agent skill level, then this can be rewritten as $P_T = k[S_1 + S_2(1 - kS_1)]$. Further, if the average skill level across all agents is S, then $(S_1 + S_2)/2 = S$. Combining these gives $P_T = k[S_1 + (2S - S_1)(1 - kS_1)] = k(2S - 2S\,kS_1 + kS_1{}^2)$. When the skill levels at layer 1 and layer 2 are equal to the average value, S, then $S_1 = S_2 = S$ and $P_T{}^* = k[S + S(1 - kS)] = k(2S - kS_2)$, where the asterisk indicates the case where skill levels are equal. Taking the difference between the two expressions for total probability gives $P_T - P_T{}^* = k(S^2 - 2SS_1 + S_1{}^2) = k(S - S_1)^2$. Because this is a squared term, it is always positive, indicating that the total probability when individual layer probabilities are different from each other is always greater than when the individual layer probabilities are uniform.

included in RMAT. This validation was based on a combination of airport planning and design guidance (Transportation Research Board, 2010; Kazda and Caves, 2007), aviation security guidance and procedures (TSA, 2006a, 2006b, 2008b, 2009c, 2011), and subject matter expert input.

Our validation found that, for the most part, the world characteristics as modeled in RMAT simulate the actual aviation system well. We also identified errors in how employee screening is modeled, though we expect that these errors would not have a significant effect on model outcomes. We also identified a number of relatively minor errors and shortcomings that could influence outcomes in RMAT. TSA has requested that we not detail these errors in this report.

RMAT represents "employee screening" through which all employees with access to the sterile area must pass. The employee screening process in RMAT is less thorough than for passenger screening. People are screened with a hand-held magnetometer instead of a walk-through metal detector or body scanner, and carry-on bags are screened with a hand-held explosives trace detector instead of X-ray and (nonportable) ETDS.

Security experts indicated that the actual employee screening process differs in two important ways. First, there is rarely a separate employee screening checkpoint; employees and passengers usually pass through the same screening checkpoint and are subjected to the same screening procedures. Second, not all employees with access to the sterile area are screened. Flight crews and tenants using retail space in the sterile area are screened. However, all other employees with access to the sterile area are exempt from security screening. This includes security staff (TSA, airport, local law enforcement, private security), government employees, airport managers, gate agents, facilities staff, cleaning crews, maintenance workers, and outside contractors.

Although important in terms of deviating from reality, this discrepancy affects only employees accessing the sterile area through the terminal. It does not affect workers accessing the AOA from the street, such as those involved in aircraft or ground maintenance, construction, freight processing, catering, or emergency response, all of which RMAT correctly models as not being screened. Because many employees have access to the sterile area with no screening, any of the insider-assisted attacks can be correctly simulated assuming no employee screening. Consequently, inaccuracies in how RMAT models screening of employees entering the sterile area through the terminal probably have little or no effect on model outcomes.

Weapon-Target Pairings and Attack Pathways

RMAT is designed to allow for new weapon-target pairings (attack types) and attack pathways to be introduced as needed. We evaluated the current suite of attack options, which chiefly represent data inputs to the model. The selection of weapon-target pairings and available attack pathways considered in RMAT is based primarily on the views of subject matter experts and the historical record of successful, failed, and planned attacks on the aviation system. RMAT has several broad categories of attack:

- hijack an airplane and crash into a building
- place a bomb on an airplane
- carry out a stand-off attack on plane (missile, rocket-propelled grenade [RPG], or high-caliber rifle)
- detonate a truck bomb against a plane at the gate
- conduct a lobby attack (abandoned bomb in terminal, suicide bomb, truck bomb at curbside check-in, shooting).

Note that whether RMAT includes all feasible weapon-target pairings and attack pathways is more than a question of its simply being comprehensive. RMAT simulates risk to the entire aviation system, which includes the adversary's ability to select the most attractive attack type. To the extent that plausible attack types are not made available to the adversary, the model will misrepresent risk by forcing the adversary to choose a nonoptimum attack type that will have greater or lesser attractiveness and consequences. Certainly modeling only one or two attack types would not realistically simulate the adaptability of an adversary. Of course, no model can hope to accurately characterize the entire spectrum of aviation security threats. But it is important to endeavor to include as much of the feasible range of options as possible.

We validated the suite of attacks modeled in RMAT by soliciting expert opinion about attacks included in RMAT and proposed alternative attacks not included in RMAT. Our validation found that the RMAT attack suite is in good alignment with views from security experts. Only a few proposed additions or changes were identified.

Each attack type requires a specific path to succeed. To verify that the paths represented in RMAT were comprehensive, we presented the paths for each attack type to subject matter experts and requested feedback.

Hijack a Passenger Plane. To hijack a passenger plane, RMAT assumes that the terrorist brings a weapon of some type on the plane. This requires taking a weapon through the checkpoint or having an insider provide the weapon to a passenger after the checkpoint. Experts commented that there was no need to use a weapon for a hijacking because it is possible to construct a weapon out of objects in the plane (e.g., make a blade from a soft drink can, wine bottles, coffee pots, fire extinguishers). If an external weapon is not needed, then RMAT incorrectly overestimates the benefit of improved passenger screening on decreasing the hijacking risk. It seems likely that the truth lies somewhere in between—external weapons are not necessary but would be more effective. RMAT could include a separate version of the hijacking scenario in which the adversary does not bring a weapon on board but rather uses an object on the plane as a weapon.

Experts also noted that, regardless of what weapon is used, the most important "weapons" in the 9/11 attacks were surprise and easy access to the cockpit, both of which are gone now. RMAT accounts for this by granting passengers and crew some chance of subduing a hijacker and of hijackers' penetrating the cockpit.

Experts also noted that it is possible for insiders themselves to board planes and take an empty seat. This would not differ significantly from an insider passing a weapon to a passenger, however, so probably would not affect the accuracy of RMAT.

Finally, RMAT does not include a pathway in which an adversary bypasses the passenger-screening checkpoint by entering the sterile area through the sterile area exit lane. Experts had mixed perceptions on the possibility of this pathway. One claimed that such a pathway is very vulnerable in certain airports where visibility is poor in crowded conditions and cited examples of this occurring, both accidentally and deliberately. Another felt this was not a significant vulnerability. A recent report (Stoller, 2011) indicated that this does occur, and hence neglecting it is a possible deficiency.

Hijack a Freight Plane. RMAT assumes that to hijack a freight plane, the terrorist must have insider access. Experts felt that this was an accurate assumption and noted a case when this happened in the past with a disgruntled employee. They felt that this was a particularly high risk, given that crews are not screened, and that it would be relatively easy to subdue any interference from the small number of people on a freight plane.

Place a Bomb on a Passenger Plane. In RMAT, a bomb can be placed on a passenger plane by smuggling the bomb (or components) through the checkpoint, having it delivered to a passenger in the sterile area by an insider, hiding it in checked luggage, or hiding it in freight. Bomb components entering the passenger compartment could be delivered by an insider or taken through a checkpoint and assembled before boarding or even on the plane.

Experts confirmed these pathways but identified two additional pathways for a bomb to reach an airplane. The first is to deliver a bomb to the aircraft belly—either as luggage or as cargo—by someone coming from a shared aviation facility with easy access to the AOA. Experts noted that many airports have military, other government (e.g., U.S. Forest Service), general aviation, and freight facilities adjacent to the commercial AOA. In many cases, the only barrier to the commercial AOA is, as noted previously, a line on the tarmac. An unscreened adversary could transport a bomb from one of these adjacent areas to a baggage or cargo tug or directly onto a commercial airplane. Experts viewed this "backdoor" pathway as high risk. Although similar to some insider-assisted attacks, this pathway differs in that is does not depend on any insiders but does require unauthorized access to the AOA.

The second pathway entails smuggling a bomb into the sterile area in vendor merchandise. An adversary could take a job with a supplier or delivery company that provides merchandise to shops or restaurants inside the sterile area and smuggle a bomb into a package. An accomplice in the sterile area could then retrieve the package and carry it onto a plane.[3] While merchandise entering the sterile area is required to be screened, not every individual item is X-rayed or hand-searched. For example, "factory packaged" items are not opened. Experts emphasized that this was also a high-risk pathway.

Place a Bomb on a Freight Plane. In RMAT, a bomb can reach a freight plane either by being in shipped freight or by being placed by an insider. Experts thought these paths were complete and accurate.

Attack with Stand-Off Weapons. RMAT includes attacks on airplanes from missiles, RPGs, and high-caliber rifles, together referred to as stand-off weapons. Stand-off weapons are assumed to be fired from an off-airport location. RMAT does not have any security barriers for a stand-off weapon attack on an airplane. Experts considered this to be accurate.

Use a Truck Bomb Against a Plane at the Gate. RMAT models a fuel truck being used as an incendiary truck bomb against an aircraft by an insider. Experts believed this to be an accurate and representative path.

Conduct a Lobby Attack. In RMAT, the lobby can be attacked by means of an abandoned bomb, a truck bomb, a suicide bomb, and light automatic weapons. Experts thought these paths were complete and accurate.

Create Diversions. RMAT does not include any type of diversion tactics to help facilitate an attack. The subject matter experts felt that deliberate diversions (e.g., climbing or driving through a perimeter fence, starting a fight, setting off a fire alarm) are an important vulnerability in that they could decrease the effectiveness of blue systems. Diversions could provide another effective path for many of these weapon-target pairs. On the other hand, diversions may increase the alertness and raise the vigilance of blue agents.

---

[3] This differs from the insider-assisted attack currently in RMAT in that in the RMAT version the insider is an airport or airline employee, who is subject to a background check, whereas in this version the employee is unaffiliated with the airport or airlines.

Weapon-Target Pairings Not Included in RMAT

We also asked experts about possible weapon-target pairings that are not included in RMAT. Additional weapon-target pairings were compiled from various sources, including TSSRA, Aviation Model Risk Assessment, and other sources. Experts were asked to comment on the relevance of these additional weapon-target pairings relative to those in RMAT, as well as on whether there were any other weapon-target pairings that they felt should be considered.

The results of this exercise identified a small number of scenarios that should be added to those in RMAT, either because they are considered important threats in TSSRA or because the experts with whom we consulted suggested that they represented important risks. As these scenarios represent potential system vulnerabilities, TSA requested that we not identify them explicitly in this report.

Attack Consequences

Each attack type modeled in RMAT has associated with it particular consequences (also referred to as effects). Attack consequences are used in RMAT in two ways. First, the adversary uses estimates of consequences as part of its computation of the attractiveness of different types of attacks. Second, the change in consequences resulting from a decrease in the probability of success is used as the measure of benefit when assessing the effectiveness of alternative security options.

Consequences in RMAT consist of three main components: deaths, direct dollars, and indirect dollars. Direct dollars include property damage, which consists of airplanes, buildings destroyed by hijacked airplanes, and aviation infrastructure destroyed by airport bombings, plus short-term business loss from aviation system shutdowns. Indirect dollars are intended to reflect the long-term losses from decreased commercial aviation business.

RMAT simulates separate consequence values for different attack outcomes. For example, a hijack may not result in the intended building-impact, but the plane and its passengers may still be lost. In this case, the deaths of building occupants and the building value are not included in the consequence estimate. Similarly, in cases where an airplane survives a bomb or stand-off attack, few deaths occur and the airplane losses are less than that for a total loss.

In RMAT, the defender's and adversary's estimates of consequences differ from each other. Specifically, the adversary values property at the replacement value, and the defender uses a substantially depreciated property value. We are not aware of any convincing support for such an assumption, but at the same time there is no reason to believe that defender and adversary valuations should necessarily be equal. Further, the importance of consequences is in distinguishing the relative attractiveness of different planned attacks and the relative loss from different completed attacks. To a first approximation, changing attractiveness values for all attacks uniformly would not change the relative attractiveness of individual attacks, nor would changing loss values for all attacks uniformly change the relative loss of individual attacks.

In addition, the adversary's perception of the indirect costs of an attack is higher than that of the defender. The rationale for the higher value is to capture the impact of the attack beyond the commercial aviation system and to reflect the adversary's desire to inflict damage on the wider society. For deaths and losses from short-term aviation system shutdown , the adversary values are equal to the defender values.

We validated consequence values in RMAT at two levels. The first was to assess whether consequence components included in RMAT are appropriate and complete. The second was to assess the accuracy of consequence values.

Consequence Components
In considering deaths, property loss, short-term business interruption, and long-term business losses, RMAT simulates most of the major categories of consequences expected from terrorist attacks on the aviation system.

The only relevant consequence category we identified that is not captured in RMAT is nonfatal injuries. Injuries in terrorist attacks are clearly an important consequence in terms of response operations, care and recovery needs, and psychological impacts. However, as discussed below, our analysis suggests that including injuries would have only a minor impact on the monetary consequences.

The consequences from injuries depends on the number of injuries anticipated and the monetized value of those injuries. Wilson et al. (2007) report that the average numbers of fatalities and injuries for all terrorist attacks in the RAND–Memorial Institute for the Prevention of Terrorism (MIPT) Terrorism Incident Database are approximately 1.5 fatalities and 3.4 injuries per attack, or about two injuries for each fatality. Terrorist attacks on the aviation system differ from terrorist attacks overall in that they tend to be more catastrophic, resulting in higher ratios of fatalities to injuries. For example, a successful bombing of an airplane will generally kill all aboard and injure few. To explore the potential impact of including injuries on RMAT results, we assume that there is one injury for every fatality.

For the monetary value of nonfatal injuries, we draw on an analysis by Willis and LaTourrette (2008) who estimated the distribution of terrorist attack injuries by severity and several alternatives for monetizing those injuries. As with the estimate from Wilson et al. (2007), this analysis was for all terrorist attacks. However, it is less obvious that the distribution of injury severity for aviation attacks will differ significantly from that for average attacks, so we make no adjustment. Using injury severity classifications adapted from the workers' compensation insurance industry, Willis and LaTourrette (2008) found that injury severity distributions were strongly skewed, with a peak at minor injuries and decreasing proportions for increasingly severe injuries: 85 percent medical only, 9 percent temporary total disability, 3 percent minor permanent partial disability, 2 percent major permanent partial disability, and 1 percent permanent total disability.

Using different health valuation methods, Willis and LaTourrette (2008) developed three sets of costs for each injury severity. Applying the method with the highest cost values to the above severity distribution gives a cost of $73,000 per injury. This is just 1 percent of the monetary value for fatalities used in RMAT ($7,000,000). Further, for most attack types, deaths are a relatively small fraction of total attack consequences. If there is one injury for every fatality, including injury costs increases total consequence values by at most 1 percent and much more typically by 0.1 percent to 0.2 percent.

Consequence Values

RMAT consequence estimates were validated by comparing them to estimates derived from the literature. Some values, such as the list price for commercial airplanes, are simple to verify. Others were more difficult and for several of the consequence components we were unable to find independent estimates.

Property. The airplane values require little discussion. We confirmed the values in RMAT by checking Boeing list prices (Boeing, undated). The only difference is in the value of the 747 freighter, which is about 14 percent higher than the value used in RMAT. This difference may reflect a difference in airplane configuration or a price increase since the RMAT consequence values were last updated. Although actual sales prices may differ from list prices, we do not consider such differences materially important for RMAT model results. We were unable to find estimates of losses to airplanes damaged (but not destroyed) by bombs or stand-off weapons, though RMAT estimates of these costs all seem plausible.

The value for a building destroyed by hijacked airplane used as a weapon in RMAT is consistent with our independent estimate. Carroll et al. (2005) compiled the insured value of buildings plus contents for the 454 largest office buildings in the U.S. These values range from $160 million to over $2,800 million with a mean of about $600 million. An iconic building in a major metropolitan area was valued at $2,668 million. Thus, the RMAT value is broadly consistent with Carroll et al. (2005).

We were unable to find independent estimates for property damage from terrorist bombing or shooting attacks. RMAT uses the same airport infrastructure property loss estimate for an abandoned bomb in an airport terminal, a curbside truck bomb, and a truck bomb against aircraft at gate. It is our judgment that the loss from a terminal bomb would typically be considerably less than that for truck bomb attacks. While the magnitude of property damage from a bombing will depend on many factors, one very important factor is the amount of explosive used. A truck bomb can contain a much larger quantity of explosives and is therefore expected to cause much greater property damage, even accounting for the fact that it is detonated outside the terminal.

Deaths. The value used in RMAT for a death caused by a terrorist attack ($7 million) is consistent with the most recent estimates for the "value of a statistical life" reported by Viscusi (2008). The value of a statistical life is derived from studies of peoples' willingness to pay for lower fatality risks, which is the preferred method for valuing lives for the purposes of government regulatory analysis (Office of Management and Budget, 2003). A complication with the willingness to pay method is that peoples' perception of risk depends on the details of the risk being considered. For example, people perceive relatively higher risks from events that are dreaded, unfamiliar, or beyond their control (Slovic, 1987). Thus, people are willing to pay more to reduce some types of risks and hence place a higher value on a statistical life for those risks. In particular, there is evidence that the appropriate value of a statistical life for deaths caused by terrorism is higher than for other risks, perhaps as much as twice the current $7 million value (Robinson et al., 2010; Viscusi, 2009). Deaths constitute a substantial fraction of total consequences in RMAT (between about 10 percent and 35 percent for most scenarios), and hence doubling the value for deaths would have a significant impact on RMAT outcomes.

The number of deaths in destroyed airplanes is consistent with the capacities of the planes (occupied at 80 percent of capacity). We could not find independent estimates of the numbers of deaths associated with partial successes, though find no reason to believe the values in RMAT are incorrect. The number of deaths in a building destroyed by a hijacked airplane (780) is within the range for buildings compiled by Carroll et al. (2005; 500–2,600), although it is low relative to the number expected for a $2,000 million building. A more appropriate number of deaths for such a building would be approximately 1,500–2,000 if all occupants were lost in the attack. As seen on 9/11, many occupants can survive building attacks, however. Therefore, the RMAT estimate is plausible but not subject to rigorous validation.

Our validation suggests that RMAT may overestimate the numbers of deaths for airport attacks. Although the variation in numbers of deaths from terrorist bombings is large, historical analyses find that suicide bombings typically kill fewer than ten people (LaTourrette et al., 2006; Hiss and Kahana, 1998), far less than the RMAT estimate of 50. Similarly, abandoned bombs have historically killed about five, even when considering only bombings that resulted in at least one injury (Bogen and Jones, 2006). Vehicle bombs may be more lethal (average of 36 fatalities per incident; LaTourrette et al., 2006). Finally, despite such high-profile examples as the 2008 Mumbai attack, terrorist shootings typically kill one or two victims (Bogen and Jones, 2006; LaTourrette et al., 2006). These historical observations are factors of 5–20 less than the RMAT estimates. Consequently, we find that the estimated numbers of deaths in RMAT in terminal attacks are unreasonably high.

Short-Term Shutdown of National Commercial Aviation System. The cost per day to the aviation industry of a complete shutdown of the commercial aviation system in the United States can be estimated from revenue lost from passenger airfares and air freight fees. There were 620 million passenger enplanements, equivalent to 310 million round-trips, on commercial aviation flights in 2010 (Bureau of Transportation Statistics, undated-a). This equates to 849,000 round-trips per day. At an average airfare of $337 per round-trip in 2010 (Bureau of Transportation Statistics, undated-a), this comes out to $286 million per day. There were 23 million tons of air cargo shipped on U.S. air carriers in 2010 (Bureau of Transportation Statistics, undated-b), or 126 million pounds per day. At an average freight fee of about $2 per pound (UPS, 2011), this comes out to $252 million per day. Summing passenger and freight losses gives $538 million per day, remarkably close to the RMAT value of $525 million per day.

The number of days that the U.S. commercial aviation system might be shut down after an attack can be estimated from the experience of the 9/11 attacks, in which the system was shut down for three days. If we assume that the shutdown duration scales linearly with the number of parallel attacks, this gives a shutdown duration of one day per parallel attack. RMAT uses half of this value for hijackings and lower values for bombing and stand-off weapon attacks. Although these values are lower than experienced on 9/11, other incidents, such as the 1988 bombing of the Pan Am flight over Lockerbie, Scotland, resulted in no shutdown. Given the very limited experience with aviation system shutdowns, there is tremendous uncertainty about what will happen in the future. Consequently, the values used in RMAT appear appropriate.

Long-Term Indirect Losses. The indirect losses in RMAT are intended to represent long-term losses in passenger revenue resulting from the ensuing decline in enplanements caused by a terrorist incident. The basis for this decline is the behavior observed after the 9/11 attacks, which resulted from a combination of fear and aversion to the increased security burdens following the terrorist attack (Peterson et al., 2007). As with direct losses, indirect losses in RMAT are accrued per parallel attack. In cases of multiple parallel attacks, the total indirect loss is the sum of the individual parallel attack values up to a maximum of four times this value for four or more parallel attacks. The rationale for capping the indirect loss at four times the parallel attack value is that with four attacks, the shock value and associated indirect losses have been maximized.

Conceptually, it is plausible that indirect losses would initially scale with parallel attacks and then decouple from them at some point. Nonetheless, capping indirect losses at the particular value of four is an arbitrary artifact of the 9/11 attacks, which happened to consist of four parallel attacks. Because indirect losses are so large and dominate total losses, the difference between capping indirect losses at four parallel attacks and, say, three or five parallel attacks would be quite substantial. Indirect loss is therefore very sensitive to the number of parallel attacks at which it is capped, and RMAT outcomes could differ significantly if this value were changed. Given that there is no compelling case to set this cap at four, a more defensible modeling approach would be to assign this value for each Monte Carlo run by drawing from a distribution that spans a feasible range of values.

For most types of airplane attacks, RMAT uses an indirect loss value of $11.1 billion per parallel attack, which is based on an estimate of $44 billion for the 9/11 attacks (Korol, 2008). Other types of attacks have lower values. We compared this $11.1 billion estimate to those of Gordon et al. (2007), who used a general equilibrium modeling approach to estimate the indirect loss over the two years following the 9/11 attacks. The analysis depends on some important assumptions, and they present multiple estimates using increasingly comprehensive assumptions. When considering only the loss from reduced airline ticket sales, they estimate a loss of approximately $42 billion. This gives an indirect loss of $10.5 billion per parallel attack, which agrees well with the RMAT value. When also accounting for losses to ground transportation, lodging, food, gifts/shopping, and amusement plus a 5 percent increase in telecommunications spending associated with each forgone airplane trip, the estimate rises to $145 billion, or $36 billion per parallel attack. When including losses to suppliers and vendors in the associated expenditure sectors, the estimate rises further to $253 billion ($63 billion per parallel attack). Finally, when considering reduced spending by households with members employed in any of the directly or indirectly affected industries, the losses amount to $399 billion ($100 billion per parallel attack).

To the extent that the indirect losses in RMAT are intended to reflect losses only to the commercial aviation industry, the values are in good agreement with the results of Gordon et al. (2007). At the same time, it seems clear that indirect losses are not restricted to the commercial aviation industry, and when considering other losses associated with reduced flying, the indirect loss estimates could be as much as a factor of 10 greater. This is a parameter that should be treated as subject to considerable uncertainty, and the implications of different ranges of values for model results should be explored.

On the other hand, an important shortcoming of the Gordon et al. (2007) analysis is that it neglects nearly all substitution effects. That is, aside from a small increase in telecommunications spending, it assumes that income lost from the decrease in commercial airline business completely disappears rather than some of it getting shifted elsewhere in the economy. This type of substitution is well known to economists and is an important reason that large, economically diverse nations are able to withstand and recover from large economic shocks (e.g., Sandler and Enders, 2008; Frey, Luechinger, and Stutzer, 2007).

Because such effects span multiple sectors across the economy, they are difficult to observe and estimate. Rose et al. (2009) developed a general equilibrium model that accounts for cross-sector substitution to estimate the indirect losses from the 9/11 attacks. They find that the total business interruption loss to the U.S. economy was just over $100 billion, which is far less than the $400 billion estimate by Gordon et al. (2007). Our understanding is poor of how spending in response to disasters shifts and substitutes among sectors, and uncertainties are great. Although the magnitude of such effects is poorly constrained, it is clear that actual indirect losses must consider both losses and gains to affected industries and sectors.

In neglecting losses beyond airfares associated with reduced commercial air travel, RMAT underestimates indirect losses. In neglecting substitution effects, RMAT overestimates indirect losses. The magnitudes of these effects are unknown, but given the magnitude of indirect losses overall, they are expected to be substantial. Consequently, there is great uncertainty in the consequence estimates in RMAT and these warrant more exploration in terms of their impact on model outcomes.

Defender Model: Satisfaction of TSA Requirements

As discussed in Chapter One, the various stakeholders in aviation security have several overlapping sets of requirements for aviation security risk analysis. Five of these are high- or medium-priority requirements that the RMAT defender model might address. Table 3.1 summarizes RMAT usefulness in meeting these requirements.

Requirement 3, stipulating how risk should be conceptualized, is partially satisfied. Attack consequences are quantified in terms of deaths, direct economic losses, and indirect economic losses. However, RMAT does not define an explicit time period over which expected losses apply. Rather, it simulates a single attack attempt, and the time period required for this attack varies from case to case. Furthermore, time in the model is not calibrated to be representative of time in the real world. Hence, RMAT provides estimates of the relative likelihoods of different attack types conditional on an attack occurring, but it is

Table 3.1
RMAT Defender Model Satisfaction of Associated TSA Requirements

Requirement	Short Description	RMAT Satisfaction of Requirement
3	Risk should be specified as the product of adversary success probability and consequences over some time period.	Partial
10	Risk assessments must identify vulnerabilities associated with portions of the domestic, commercial air transportation system.	Partial
11	Risk assessments should represent threats described by TSSRA and others.	Partial
13	Risk assessment methods should describe the risk benefits of existing and planned security systems.	Yes
14	Risk assessments should account for performance heterogeneity in security systems.	Partial

not designed to express probability or losses in the conventional units of incidents or expected losses per time interval.

Requirement 10, which concerns the scope of vulnerabilities considered by risk analyses, is partially satisfied. In general, RMAT faithfully simulates the characteristics of the U.S. commercial aviation system; the procedures, staffing, and instrumentation used to secure it; and the major vulnerabilities to it. We identified several correctable errors in the world representation, most of which are minor and are expected to have little impact on model outcomes. However, because a large part of the aviation security threat stems from U.S.-bound international flights, the fact that RMAT does not simulate security on such flights is an important shortcoming.

Requirement 11 concerns the threats considered in risk analyses. We find that this requirement is partially satisfied. RMAT simulates most, but not all, of the security threats described in the TSSRA. TSSRA, for instance, counts chemical and biological attacks as high-risk scenarios, but these are not included among the current set of RMAT attacks. Further, some important attack pathways are not included, such as unauthorized access to secure areas and some high-risk insider-assisted pathways. By failing to include these pathways, RMAT may underestimate the risk of a bomb attack on an airplane.

Requirement 13 calls for methods to estimate the risks and benefits associated with new or candidate security procedures. RMAT has been designed to produce such estimates, and we consider the validity of those estimates elsewhere, so we consider this requirement to have been met. RMAT accounts for the combined security operations of multiple organizations and is consistent with most plans, programs, policies, and procedures. In addition, RMAT accounts for the cumulative effects of multiple security measures operating simultaneously.

Requirement 14 notes the importance of risk analysis acknowledging heterogeneity in defender performance. Heterogeneity resulting from partial deployment of security measures can be addressed by allowing the user to select the probability that an adversary will encounter a particular measure during reconnaissance and attacks. Also, RMAT does allow blue agent skill level to be varied among agent types and from one Monte Carlo run to the next, but it does not allow heterogeneity in skill level among blue agents of a given type within a single run. Such intrarun heterogeneity can influence model outcomes.

Recommendations for Revisions to the RMAT Defender Model

In general, RMAT has an accurate representation of airport security processes, but some improvements could further strengthen the RMAT characterization of air transportation system risks.

Address differences in security screening between domestic and foreign airports. RMAT currently models security using a single abstraction of the U.S. commercial aviation system. Consequently, it does not capture differences in security among different airports. One of the most important of these differences is that between domestic and foreign airports. Aviation systems of other nations do not conform to the same security standards as those in the United States, and security may differ from country to country. Given the current structure of RMAT, accounting for security differences at foreign airports may not be straightforward. One possible approach would be to distinguish separate attack types for international flights that use distinct instruments, staffing, and parameter values relevant to security at foreign airports. TSA and Boeing recognize the importance of incorporating foreign flights into the domestic system and have plans to adapt RMAT to include them.

Include attack pathways that exploit the probability that credentials will not always be checked. RMAT requires that agents always possess the necessary credentials to move within the world and does not include any attack scenarios that entail entering locations without the proper credential. However, our analysis revealed that there are attack pathways in which credentials are not always checked. Including such pathways, with the appropriate probability that a credential would be checked would strengthen RMAT.

Add additional attack scenarios. While RMAT has a wide variety of attack types, there are some that are high-priority threats in TSSRA that are not in RMAT. These should be added in order of perceived importance. Additionally, we identified two other scenarios that should be considered for inclusion. The specifics of these scenarios are security-sensitive so are not described in this report.

Decrease deaths for terminal attacks. Our validation found that RMAT may overestimate the number of deaths in airport terminal attacks. Judging by outcomes of past attacks, we find that the number of deaths in such attacks should be reduced by factors of 5–20.

Account for uncertainty in consequence values. Our validation identified some important uncertainties in the consequences from aviation terrorism that are not adequately conveyed in the way RMAT is designed and how it handles uncertainty. One important uncertainty is the value of a statistical life. RMAT uses the currently accepted value of $7 million. However, emerging research suggests that the appropriate valuation of life associated with terrorism may be as much as a factor of two higher. Research in this area is ongoing and there is no consensus on the best value. Including an option to vary this value would allow users to examine the effect of differing assumptions.

There are other, more substantial, uncertainties associated with the indirect losses. The first has to do with the relationship between indirect losses and the number of parallel attacks. The current assumption that indirect losses do not increase with the number of parallel attacks beyond four parallel attacks, while plausible, is an arbitrary choice stemming from the 9/11 attacks. Varying the number of parallel attacks at which indirect losses are capped would influence the number of parallel attacks that is most attractive to an adversary and the total consequences for an attack. These changes would affect which attacks are attempted as well as the benefit of security measures that prevent them.

A second important uncertainty in estimating indirect losses is the amount of loss beyond airfares from forgone flights associated with a decline in commercial aviation business. The indirect loss in RMAT is intended to represent losses to the commercial aviation system, and our validation finds that the RMAT value of $11 billion is consistent with the decrease in airline ticket sales for the two years following 9/11. However, we also found that, when considering losses to service sectors associated with commercial aviation, airline tickets may represent as little as 10 percent of the total loss stemming from decreased air travel. Indirect losses could therefore arguably be as much as ten times greater than the RMAT estimate.

A final uncertainty that pushes indirect losses in the opposite direction is the extent to which other types of spending substitute for decreased spending from forgone air travel. Although there is reliable evidence that this substitution effect occurs, there is little empirical basis for estimating its magnitude. More research is needed to understand how consumer spending shifts in response to fear, hassle, and other impediments to commercial air travel after terrorist attacks.

To some extent, these uncertainties could be characterized simply as limitations in available data, and users could explore a range of values for each uncertain parameter. However, our analysis suggests that consequence values will always be too uncertain to develop reliable or meaningful point estimates. As a result, we recommend that RMAT be revised to more explicitly incorporate uncertainty analysis in its architecture.

CHAPTER FOUR

RMAT Data Requirements and Sources

RMAT has thousands of input variables, which places heavy demands on the identification and validation of accurate parameter values quantifying aspects of airports, security operations, terrorist operations, and attack outcomes and their valuation. To fulfill model data requirements, Boeing and TSA have undertaken extensive and repeated data collection efforts. These collection efforts have relied on elicitations with subject matter experts, assessments of technical and scientific data, review of TSA policies and procedures, and other data sources. Because the model, the system it describes, and threats to it are constantly evolving, the validity of RMAT results depends on the reliability and validity of ongoing data collection efforts. This chapter explores the validity of data sources used as inputs to the RMAT model, the rigor and reliability of the data collection processes that have been used, and the compliance of these processes with RMAT requirements.

Quantity and Types of Data

RMAT includes input data that describe the adversary, blue agents, credentials, perception enhancers, materials, material detectors, weapons, and attack types. Each of these broad categories contains specific types of objects and each type has many characteristics that are defined by inputs. These characteristics are similar for each type within a category. In Table 4.1, we have tabulated by category the number of types and inputs per type. At the time of this study, there were 4,182 inputs

Table 4.1
Input Count for Model Objects by Category

	Types	Inputs per Type	Total
Adversary	3	114	342
Blue agents	35	9	315
Credentials	21	3	63
Perception enhancers	6	2	12
Materials	15	4	60
Material detectors	14	8	112
Weapons	88	26	2,288
Attack types	66	15	990
Total			4,182

related to these categories, though this number will grow as RMAT adds more scenarios and aspects to the model.

Table 4.1 is only a partial count of the data inputs because there are other parameters that do not describe these broad classes of objects in the model. These other inputs include 161 inputs from a "configuration constant" file. These additional parameters adjust some of the model functions. The configuration constants include both substantive assumptions about the system's response and technical parameters with little impact on the results.

A conservative estimate for the number of inputs would be 4,343 (4,182 + 161). In addition, however, there are numerous agent behaviors and parameters that have been hard-coded into the software, which could also be considered parameters subject to change. The RAND study team had only limited access to the code, so we could not determine how many such hard-coded parameter estimates there are.

Validation

The scale of the data used in the model made a complete validation impossible within the project's time line; instead, we used statistical sampling to draw inferences about the full set of input values, based on observations from a subsample selected probabilistically. Because of the large number of inputs for each adversary object, we randomly sampled from the adversary inputs instead of sampling from the objects themselves. The objects and parameters were weighted by their importance on the model's output and then sampled randomly. Importance values reflected the frequency with which parameters were used in major RMAT functions. Using this weighted stratified sampling design, we sampled 130 inputs for in-depth validation. From a statistical standpoint, this sample size provides better than a 95 percent chance of finding two or more invalid inputs if 5 percent or more of the inputs are invalid.

Several of the selected parameters have been assigned values that are security-sensitive or not publicly releasable. Our validation efforts sought to confirm the legitimacy of these inputs too, though their values will not be discussed here.

We considered diverse forms of evidence to validate the data, including logic, subject matter expert judgments, and literature searches. We could validate some parameter values on logical or definitional grounds. For example, nonmetallic knives are not explosive and need not contain any metal, so we could logically confirm values assigned to them on parameters describing their explosive force potential and their metal content (related to their detectability by magnetometers). For the other inputs, we searched relevant literature and consulted with subject matter experts to validate the value. Subject matter experts included terrorism experts and airport security personnel. We sought manufacturer specifications, news reports, and peer-reviewed articles as literature sources. For some inputs, we could not find sufficient information to confirm or disconfirm the RMAT value. The summary of these findings can be found in Table 4.2. We combined materials, material detectors, and perception enhancers together as equipment for the purpose of the validation.

Table 4.2
Independent Confirmation Results for Sampled Parameters

	Total Sampled	Confirmed	Disconfirmed	Not Estimable	Unconfirmable
Adversary	20	11	4	0	5
Blue agent	18	12	0	6	0
Credentials	3	0	3	0	0
Attack types	30	12	0	4	14
Equipment	6	3	0	0	3
Weapon	52	35	0	3	14
Configuration	1	0	1	0	0
Total	130	73	8	13	36

Those parameter values for which we found neither confirming nor disconfirming evidence, we list in Table 4.2 as "unconfirmable." In addition, however, we classed some variables as "not estimable," when, in consultation with former intelligence analysts and aviation subject matter experts, we concluded that the information required to estimate the variable either does not exist or is subject to such profound sources of uncertainty that we judged they could not reasonably be estimated. Examples of such parameters include those used to estimate the terrorist's perception of the diminishing returns on each additional parallel attack, the parameter that dictates how rapidly the adversary can update its knowledge of security systems, and the parameters terrorists would apply to candidate attacks for purposes of judging their relative attractiveness. These and other RMAT parameters require information beyond what intelligence or academic research can credibly provide.

Excessive reliance on parameters that are not measurable, particularly for parameters that have a strong impact on the results, can result in assumption-driven outcomes. These inputs should undergo extensive sensitivity testing so that their impact on model results is well understood and these uncertainties can be conveyed to policymakers.

Similarly, many parameters have a standard deviation as an input in addition to a mean value. This assumes a known distribution for the underlying parameter, which is not true for many of the inputs. When a distribution is not known, it is better to examine implications of the full range of plausible values, rather than sampling values from a presumed distribution.

As shown in Table 4.2, we disconfirmed eight of the 130 values we sampled (7 percent of the data when scaled to the full data set as distributed in Table 4.1). Extrapolating from our sampling plan, we can infer with a 95 percent confidence interval that between 2 percent and 11 percent of all RMAT would be disconfirmable. Moreover, an additional 9 percent of inputs appear to serve parameters that are inherently not estimable. This estimate would correspond to more than 600 variables in RMAT that are disconfirmable or not estimable. Although it is true that the subject matter experts and intelligence analysts who provided the initial values for the disconfirmed variables may have had access to information that was unavailable to us, the detailed explanation of why we classed these eight values as disconfirmed shows that in half the cases, the disconfirmed values are not ones likely to have been recommended by experts.

Adequacy of Sources

The RMAT team described a hierarchy of sources for input values, with preference given to data from the Aviation Security Assessment Program (ASAP), a program that conducts systematic red team tests of airport security systems and laboratory test data. When these sources are unavailable, the team first considers published analysis and finally subject matter expert opinions. We asked Boeing and TSA to share documentation with us on the sources they relied on to arrive at the 130 sampled values. Table 4.3 summarizes these sources. Roughly two-thirds of the sampled inputs come from subject matter experts with the remaining split between the literature, test data, and inputs that control model functions but do not correspond to confirmable events. Examples of model parameters that reflect these expert judgments include characterization of the attractiveness of targets to adversaries, the skills of potential adversaries, the rate at which potential adversaries

Table 4.3
RMAT Sources of Data on Sampled Values

	Inputs Sampled	Subject Matter Experts	Literature or Test Data	Not Applicable or Model
Adversary	20	15	0	5
Blue agent	18	18	0	0
Credentials	3	3	0	0
Effects	30	12	0	18
Equipment	8	5	0	3
Weapon	52	32	20	0
Configuration	1	1	0	0
Total	132	86	20	26

can learn new information about security systems, and the effectiveness of security measures at detecting and stopping attacks.

Of the sampled inputs, the only category of input that was documented as having used any literature sources was the weapon class, and these inputs were primarily for detectability values from TSA data. All other variable estimates were attributed to subject matter experts, though in some cases these experts may have drawn on data sources. Moreover, we sampled from the common baseline parameters. For individual case studies, TSA reports incorporating all available data from relevant ASAP studies. Although none of the variables we sampled were documented as coming from ASAP, the experts listed in the documentation may have drawn on their knowledge of ASAP data and other reliable sources.

The heavy reliance on experts highlights the importance of examining the methods used to elicit their judgments. We do so in the next section by comparing how Boeing and TSA conduct elicitations to established best practices.

How RMAT Uses Expert Elicitations

The RMAT team has incorporated multiple approaches to expert elicitation. Whereas a large number of values were elicited early in RMAT development to support the baseline case, subsequent case studies have required new elicitations that have used more sophisticated procedures.

Boeing and TSA have conducted elicitations with TSA intelligence personnel to collect values associated with attacker characteristics and with aviation security personnel for values concerning the effectiveness of security measures. Though the experts represented a variety of perspectives, and often were well suited to provide needed judgments, in some cases they were selected based on availability rather than through a process that matched experts to stated criteria for expertise. In cases where external experts were either not available or could not be identified, the elicited estimates reflect the judgments of the Boeing and TSA RMAT modeling team that were subsequently reviewed and approved by at least one TSA official.

In some cases, elicitations have involved one-on-one discussions between a member of the RMAT team and a subject matter expert. When this approach was used, the number of experts interviewed depended on how many could be identified. When more than one expert was used and elicited results did not agree, the RMAT team reached an internal consensus to resolve the disagreement.

In other cases, elicitations were conducted in small groups or larger, more formal workshops. Each of these formats incorporated an opportunity for participants to discuss the estimates provided, and participants were asked to develop a consensus judgment. In general, discussions were managed so that a single consensus estimate emerged, or an average estimate of the multiple views was calculated for the RMAT parameter. Elicitations related to the performance of technologies were generally one-on-one interviews, and those related to insight from the intelligence community were conducted as small groups or workshops.

The methods used to elicit information at times involved offering a suggested response and asking the expert to comment on whether this was an appropriate judgment. According to discussions with TSA personnel and TSA support personnel, respondents were generally asked for their best estimates and were not always asked for bounds or ranges for their estimates. Elicitation procedures have not usually been documented or standardized.

In many cases, the RMAT team reports making efforts to assess the reliability of expert judgments. In some cases, for instance, individual judgments were shared and discussed with other experts. These discussions influenced either which values TSA used in RMAT or how they combined estimates when multiple were elicited.

According to Boeing and TSA personnel, assessments performed earlier in the modeling process exhibited greater disagreement. This has been anecdotally attributed to disagreements stemming from vague and unclear wording of the elicitation questions. As elicitations continued, the RMAT team has improved the clarity of questions by documenting additional process flows, standardized elicitation documents, allowing experts to express and assess contingent dependencies that affect their judgments, and more formally incorporated approaches for providing experts feedback on their assessments. However, the elicitation processes and approaches to framing questions reportedly vary depending on the specific experts who are engaged.

Expert Elicitation Best Practices

Reliable expert elicitations generates well-calibrated and coherent estimates (Hora, 2007a, 2007b; Morgan and Henrion, 1990). Calibration refers to the accuracy of estimates. Coherence refers to whether the estimates follow logic associated with either probabilistic relationships or membership of sets and subsets. Methods of expert elicitation use three approaches to ensure reliability.

First, elicitation questions must be well specified. To the extent questions are vague, variation in interpretation by the experts leads to disagreement in judgments (Hora, 2007a). A common standard used to assess whether questions are well posed is the *omniscience test*; if the question were posed to an all-knowing person, would that person be able to answer the question as posed or would clarification be required? For example, if asked, "What is the average daily temperature?" the omniscient would need to clarify the where and when the questioner was referring to (e.g., last year's global temperature). In theory, the omniscience test is sufficient to ensure that questions are well specified.

The question used in elicitations must also be one for which there is a basis for an estimate. Grounds for a reliable answer can be a strong understanding of the underlying phenomena or experience with prior or analogous problems, either of which would allow an expert to respond reliably. For example, it is likely impossible for an expert to assess the effectiveness of a technology that has not yet been developed, will be used in a process that has not incorporated other technologies, and is not well characterized by a process model. However, it is easier for an expert to assess a known technology in a new but similar application.

Second, care is given in the selection of appropriate experts. Experts tend to produce more reliable estimates when they have either analogous experience or fundamental knowledge and when they receive feedback on the coherence and calibration of the judgments they have offered (Morgan and Henrion, 1990). Thus, expert elicitation methods give a great deal of attention to the methods used to identify experts.

Finally, gathering reliable expert elicitations requires framing questions to avoid the common judgment and decisionmaking biases of availability, overconfidence, representativeness, and anchoring and adjustment (Tversky and Kahneman, 1974).

Several protocols have been developed to achieve these outcomes and generally fall into two classes: individual elicitation methods and group processes.

Methods to elicit information from individuals. Several approaches exist for eliciting information from individual experts. Most were developed decades ago and have been applied to problems as diverse as setting air pollution standards (Wallsten and Whitfield, 1986), fate and transport of pollutants (Morgan et al., 1984), and energy facility reliability (Boyd and Regulinski, 1979). Although the details of each approach vary slightly, they each incorporate five similar steps: motivation, structuring, conditioning, encoding, and verifying.

The first three steps—motivation, structuring, and conditioning— are intended to ensure that experts

- understand the elicitation task
- are asked questions that they are comfortable with and prepared to answer

- are aware of common biases and heuristics that could limit the coherence or calibration of the elicitations.

The fourth task—encoding—involves eliciting information from experts, typically using elicitation tools and approaches designed to minimize the effects of heuristics and biases. Finally, the fifth task—verification—provides a check on whether the results of the elicitation accurately affect the experts' views. This step frequently includes opportunities for experts to reflect on elicited results that disagree with other experts or reveal poor coherence or calibration and, if desired, to adjust their answers. Incorporating these tasks into individual elicitation has been demonstrated to improve the reliability of resulting estimates (Cojazzi et al., 2001).

Methods for eliciting information from groups. In most problems of interest, experts will disagree about the value of uncertain quantities being elicited. For these situations, elicitation methods have been developed to characterize the range of opinions that exist. The rationale for eliciting from groups instead of individuals stems from the reasons that experts might disagree—of which there are several.

Experts may have different awareness or understanding of the science or statistics involved in phenomena, even when questions are stated clearly and unambiguously. Ignorance or error could lead one expert to disagree with another. Moreover, multiple valid interpretations of the science can also lead to disagreement in cases where more than one model or theory exists to explain a phenomenon. Finally, personal incentives or interests may motivate bias in answers; that in itself generates disagreement.

In each of these cases, interaction among groups can help to resolve disagreements either by clarifying the cause of the disagreement or by filling gaps in knowledge and clarifying misconceptions that the experts might have. Methods of incorporating group interaction into assessment include mathematically merging elicited results, face-to-face group discussions such as focus groups, and Delphi-type interactions that allow groups to discuss individual judgments (Morgan and Henrion, 1990).

Mathematical techniques, such as averaging elicited answers, are simple to implement and often effective at generating reliable estimates. But in cases where more than one valid viewpoint exists, mathematical techniques can provide misleading results and can obscure the sources of disagreement (Morgan and Henrion, 1990). Face-to-face group interactions offer experts an opportunity share information, question each other, and challenge each other's ideas. This approach has been shown to improve the reliability of elicited results and motivated Delphi-like approaches. However, group interactions are subject to known problems stemming from group dynamics when individual experts exert excessive influence or coercion over other participants leading to changes in elicited answers (Gustafson et al., 1973; Linstone and Turoff, 1975; and Myers and Lamm, 1975).

Other methods have been developed to achieve the benefits of group interactions while limiting the influence of persuasion and coercion. Examples of these methods include the nominal group technique (Gustafson et al., 1973) and the deliberative method for ranking risks (Florig et al., 2001). These methods begin with methods of individual elicitation and then incorporate those into tasks involving moderated group interaction facilitated to minimize the opportunity for one individual to dominate a discussion. Such approaches have been applied to health and safety risk, ecological and environmental health, and, most recently, homeland security risk management (Morgan et al., 2001; Willis et al., 2004, 2010; and Willis and Lundberg, 2011).

Comparing RMAT Elicitations to Best Practices

Comparison of the expert elicitation methods used in RMAT to best practices raises several concerns about the validity and reliability of the information contained in the RMAT model.

First, the RMAT team was not always given access to requested experts. Thus, the approaches used to identify and recruit experts appear to be driven largely by the availability of experts rather than by explicit criteria for the expertise sought and assessment of whether the individuals involved have the background and experience that would suggest they could be well-calibrated experts. Improved access and well-defined expert selection criteria would likely lead to requirements to extend RMAT elicitations to expert groups beyond those already used.

Second, the elicitation approaches used likely promote over-confidence and anchoring. For example, in cases where experts were uncertain and reluctant to hazard guesses, facilitators would reportedly suggest a possible answer as a starting point for the elicitation. Furthermore, elicitation approaches did not until recently attempt to elicit lower and upper uncertainty ranges for elicited parameters. Instead, early elicitations captured only point estimates, creating a false sense of precision where the true uncertainty range might support a wider range of results and conclusions. Elicitations reportedly now do attempt to capture lower and upper bounds. It will be important to ensure that elicitation procedures and results are formally documented.

In cases where groups are used, reported processes do not mitigate unfavorable group dynamics. For example, our study team observed elicitations where group discussions were dominated by a single individual—one who had management responsibilities for the other experts. In this case, the dominant individual was offering a highly favorable assessment of the effectiveness of the security program he managed—an assessment substantially different from that offered by his employees when they were interviewed separately. Although the discussion process can lead to a better estimate than any one member would have produced, senior experts (in particular if they have a supervisory role over other panel members) may have an undue influence over others.

Third, in cases where multiple experts were consulted, differences between their judgments were not recorded. Instead, the RMAT team used either mathematical approaches to aggregating experts' opinions (e.g., averaging answers), forced consensus among experts (a process that raises concerns about group interactions), or made a reasoned judgment about which of several proposed parameter values to accept.

RMAT Data: Satisfaction of TSA Requirements

Of the requirements identified for TSA risk assessments detailed in the appendix, one focuses on data validity and the data acquisition process (Table 4.4).

Requirement 19 emphasizes that RMAT data should be authenticated and traceable. The sample validation indicates that a small proportion of inputs to RMAT have values that are likely not correct. The sources of data values are reported, but there is little or no systematic process for maintaining additional documentation about the data collection for specific inputs. This makes it difficult to audit the data for validation purposes. In the case of expert judgment data, the methods used do not conform to the best practices for expert elicitation, meaning that they may be unreliably collected. Therefore, this requirement is only partially met.

Observations and Recommendations

RMAT uses thousands of inputs that are fed into various functions to provide assessments on terrorism risk. Roughly 7 percent of these variables may be incorrect, judging from the parameter values we sampled, and an additional 8 percent are not confirmable because the underlying attribute is not truly measurable as modeled. TSA and Boeing could implement several measures to improve the validity of model data.

Document review and modification of data collection processes. To resolve problems with disconfirmed inputs, a time line should be established to update each variable. Variables that change dramatically with additional information about current and evolving threats would need to be updated more frequently than variables that describe the phys-

Table 4.4
RMAT Data Sources Agreement with Associated TSA Requirements

Requirement	Short Description	RMAT Satisfaction of Requirements
19	Data supporting risk assessments must be authenticated and traceable.	Partial

ics or chemistry underlying some of the processes. This would increase the likelihood that RMAT is relevant to the current decisionmaking processes.

Adopt empirical expressions of uncertainty. We considered many of the inputs that could not be confirmed to be highly uncertain and should be replaced with a distribution within some range of plausible values. Currently, for parameters that range between zero and one, RMAT uses a Gaussian noise with standard deviation of 0.2 to sample some of the variables. This asserts incorrect precision; the representation should be replaced by something more characteristic of actual uncertainty justifiable from the literature or subject matter estimates.

Additionally, using a Gaussian distribution with standard deviation of 0.2 inside a bounded region will skew the resulting distribution (unless the initial value is equal to 0.5). This effect will be magnified toward the edges, so that if a variable has a default value of 1.0, the resulting sample mean will be closer to 0.92. This means that any sensitivity testing on the variables between zero and one will be biased. This is a substantive problem and can be addressed by making sure that the distribution used during the sensitivity analysis preserves the mean.

Avoid parameters that cannot in principle be estimated. Some key parameters are uncertain and cannot be avoided. That said, efforts should be made to minimize the number of immeasurable parameters included in the model. Ideally, RMAT components that rely on immeasurable inputs could be redesigned to avoid the need for these inputs. For example, the abstract defender skill level is difficult to measure (if at all possible), but actual defender performance from red team tests may be available. Thus, the complex functions defining the probability of detection might be replaced with actual data.

When parameters that cannot be estimated accurately are important to the model's conceptual validity, they should be treated as sources of deep uncertainty for the model's results. These parameters should be subjected to exploratory modeling to understand how they affect outcomes in combination with other sources of deep uncertainty (see the discussion in Chapter Six).

Align expert elicitation with best practices. By drawing on the best practices reviewed above, TSA could improve the elicitation methods used in RMAT. Specifically, the RMAT processes could be modified to

- incorporate selection criteria and recruiting procedures for engaging experts
- adopt and consistently use elicitation methods that mitigate the effects of judgment heuristics and biases and group dynamics
- represent the uncertainty that exists in elicited results and carry those uncertainties through to RMAT results.

However, before refining elicitation procedures, TSA should first consider how expert elicited values are used in RMAT. If the objective of RMAT is not to produce best estimates about future risks but rather to explore how different sources of uncertainty affect results, subject matter experts might be used to bound the plausible ranges on variables rather than to make point estimates.

Even if elicited well, parameters related to attacker preferences, attacker capabilities, and security measure effectiveness will be subject to significant uncertainty. Elicited answers can therefore be expected to reflect wide variations in viewpoints. Moreover, these views may fluctuate abruptly when new information is obtained about the intentions or capabilities of a particular individual or group. Thus, instead of considering these parameters as values to be estimated, RMAT could instead treat them as uncertainties to be analyzed through exploratory modeling.

Seek opportunities to validate subject matter expert judgments with empirical data. TSA administrators should assist in giving access to the best available data sources and experts for RMAT refinement. Too few of the inputs were generated using test data and literature sources. Whenever possible, literature sources should augment subject matter expert judgments. RMAT would also benefit from access to test data regarding the actual performance of TSO and other defender systems, including results of red-teaming experiments. The RMAT team's preference hierarchy for input data is laudable, preferring operational test data (e.g., red-teaming efforts to penetrate security) to lab data, and lab data to that provided by subject matter experts.

CHAPTER FIVE

RMAT Model Performance and Management

To produce valid and useful results, RMAT requires more than just a good conceptual model underlying its source code. It also needs code that faithfully characterizes the conceptual models and change management processes that help to ensure that the code remains faithful through periodic modifications necessary for new case studies of risk, when improvements are made to the conceptual model, or when detected errors are corrected.

Our study team was permitted to inspect the RMAT source code at Boeing's facility in Huntsville, Ala., but not to take it back to RAND where we could undertake more leisurely and in-depth analysis of the software. However, Boeing did provide RAND with an executable version of RMAT, extensive consultation on its use and interpretation, and detailed information on Boeing's software change management processes. Within these constraints, RAND approached the software validation effort in four ways:

- *Code inspection.* At Boeing's facility in Huntsville, Ala., the RAND study team conducted a cursory inspection of the source code architecture to become familiar with its organization, general characteristics, and some of the key functions. In addition, we ran software quality diagnostic tools on it.
- *Sensitivity analysis.* Using the RMAT executable file, we conducted over 25,000 RMAT trials, systematically varying 21 input variables. The sensitivity analysis was designed to establish whether the input and output variables are associated in predictable ways, thereby providing indirect evidence that the source code faith-

fully implements the conceptual models. In addition, these analyses were useful for understanding the sensitivity of model outputs to key input variables.

- *Targeted verification.* Although we could not conduct detailed verifications of many RMAT functions or modules, we attempted to verify one key RMAT function—its calculation of adversary attack attractiveness. For this analysis, we compared RMAT output to outputs we calculated using the RMAT conceptual model.
- *Change management verification.* Finally, we examined Boeing's change management processes, its evolution and plans for the process, and examples of how recent change orders were produced and executed.

Code Inspection

As software becomes lengthy and complex, it can tax the understanding of programmers charged with maintaining and modifying the code, finding errors in it, or explaining the code to others who might need to use it. As such, software best practices have evolved to improve comprehensibility, management, and, therefore, reliability (Pfleeger and Atlee, 2006). These practices emphasize

- organizing the architecture into independent functional modules, often organized hierarchically
- avoiding highly nested logic in which many layers of conditional statements occur
- using class structures to group and maintain related parameters, rather than passing large numbers of parameters to a method, since passing multiple parameters requires extensive bookkeeping on the part of the programmer and can degrade performance
- avoiding functions or modules that have a very large number of logical paths that might be difficult for programmers to understand or track

- relying on more general or abstract functions to handle similar operations rather than allowing a proliferation of similar single-application or concrete functions.

To evaluate RMAT on these and other software architecture characteristics, we used NDepend (www.ndepend.com), a commercial source code management and analysis tool that provides several code quality metrics.[1]

For RMAT, NDepend identified 58 violations of its software quality metrics. Violations and critical violations are registered when quality metrics exceed thresholds set by NDepend. Among these, NDepend identified three types of violations it classed as "critical":

- *Methods too complex.* NDepend's "complexity" score is a count of the number of logical paths that can be taken through a module (Pfleeger and Atlee, 2006). Complexity of 20 or more is scored as "hard to understand and maintain" and 40 or more as "critical." NDepend found 37 critical violations of complexity in RMAT methods. One module designing the adversary's optimal attack trajectory had a complexity of 223 and a logical nesting depth of 23.[2] The methods for building an attack plan and finding the best attack path for the adversary have complexity scores of 132 and 127, respectively.
- *Methods with too many parameters.* The "methods with too many parameters" metric measures the number of parameters that the system passes to a method when it is executed. More than five passed parameters is scored as "difficult to call" and those with

---

[1]   NDepend assumes a hierarchical architecture for the software in which the top level is the application, which comprises assemblies, which comprise namespaces, which comprise types, which comprise methods and fields.

[2]   The nesting depth is the number of "encapsulated scopes" in the method. For example, when an "IF" statement lies within another IF statement, it represents a nesting depth of two. NDepend regards nesting depths of four as difficult to understand and maintain and those greater than eight as extremely complex. The nesting depth is related to the complexity. If each encapsulation has two branches, then a module with a nesting depth of eight has 256 independent paths through it.

greater than eight as "critical." NDepend found ten methods with more than eight passed parameters and marked them as critical. We evaluated most of these violations as being of trivial importance, as they involved passing parameters to a log file for recording.

- *Types too big.* Types are collections of methods that carry out a related set of functions. The "types too big" metric counts the number of lines of code and the number of instructions in each type. NDepend identified 27 types that have more than 500 lines of code or 3,000 instructions. One type related to adversary decisionmaking has almost 4,300 lines of code, almost 26,000 instructions, and 73 methods. Another type has 693 methods. Often, large types have duplicative code and other redundancies. Consequently, maintaining the code and identifying bugs can be difficult.

Additionally, NDepend determined that RMAT is highly concrete code, potentially leading to redundancies in the code itself and making RMAT more difficult to maintain. Concreteness is the opposite of abstractness: Abstractness in software indicates the degree to which the software is a generalization of the logic being modeled. Abstract methods group common data structures and logical elements, making them easier to use and maintain than "concrete" methods, which maintain separate implementations of similar data and logic. The abstractness metric is the ratio of the number of abstract types to the total number of types, so ranges from 0 (highly concrete, single-use methods) to 1 (highly general, abstract methods). The abstractness of five of the seven major components (or assemblies) comprised by RMAT is 0. The highest value of abstractness is 0.02, and this is for the key assembly in RMAT that performs the risk-analysis logic. Some aspects of RMAT, such as the management of its execution, are justifiably concrete. In other parts of the program, specifically in the logic underlying the adversary, we expected a much higher level of abstraction. We judged three of the assemblies as properly concrete, because they manage specific, single-purpose activities.

Boeing is aware of these issues and has initiated internal actions to improve the code, independent of the NDepend analysis. We have not reviewed their proposed changes.

In summary, RMAT source code logic and organization are not transparent. Many methods are quite large and have dozens of levels of logic, making them difficult to interpret, modify, test, and manage. Many of the methods and even some parameter values are hard-coded, or scripted within the code itself, rather than abstracted into more general functions. Many methods with similar names appear to perform similar functions. There is no formal documentation of the requirements, architecture, algorithms, or end user manuals, though some areas of the code have comments. Documentation is ongoing for RMAT. Additionally, the software architecture has not, for the most part, been structured into units that can be reviewed and tested independently as is a software best practice (Pfleeger and Atlee, 2006).

These software flaws are understandable. RMAT is a first-of-a-kind system that has evolved as a prototype. It has been adapted and continuously modified to fit new requirements. The result is a complex program with substantially less organization and efficiency than would be expected of a production model, or even a prototype designed to TSA's current risk-management requirements.

As understandable as the software's current state is, it presents significant challenges for expanding, revising, debugging, testing, and managing the code, all of which threaten RMAT reliability and validity. Simple modifications can be made reliably by developers who are intimately familiar with the system. Other modifications such as a new approach for determining attack attractiveness for adversaries may be more difficult and time-consuming and have broader ramifications for RMAT and its reliability.

Sensitivity Analysis

The sensitivity analysis we performed using the RMAT executable file was designed to establish whether input variables had the expected associations with model results and to evaluate how sensitive RMAT results are to variations in parameters, some of which may not be estimated with precision.

Design of the Analysis

Input parameters. The large parameter space and relatively slow runtime in RMAT (approximately one minute per Monte Carlo trial) made a comprehensive sensitivity analysis infeasible. Instead, we identified 23 input variables that we believed should or could be influential in model results and systematically varied their values in sequential RMAT "excursions" or batches of Monte Carlo trials with the same input value settings.[3] Values on the variables were selected using a near orthogonal Latin hypercube (NOLH). Our design entailed 257 unique combinations of values on the 23 variables, with each variable being allowed to vary between "low" and "high" values. For continuous parameters, the low value was one-half of the RMAT default value, and the high value was twice the RMAT default value. For Boolean parameters, the parameter was either 0 or 1. It is important to note that the experimental approach is designed to test model sensitivity. As such, parameter values are used that might be inappropriate for evaluating security risks, and no inferences about security should be drawn from our results.

We selected the NOLH approach because it is an efficient way to explore a large parameter space. A systematic, parameter-by-parameter exploration of the input space of RMAT would have been infeasible, for several reasons. First, RMAT has thousands of parameters. Second, even for our reduced space of 21 parameters, a full factorial design of experiments would have required an infeasible number of runs, given the length of time each run requires. Finally, given that many of the

---

[3] Boeing has requested that we omit detailed descriptions of the variables we tested on grounds that the information is business proprietary. In summary, 11 variables concerned resources, preferences, capabilities, and other characteristics of the adversary; ten concerned performance characteristics of various aviation security components; and two concerned estimates of attack consequences. Two of the input parameters we selected for the sensitivity analysis turned out to have been "deprecated," meaning that the software has evolved and the parameters have been superseded by other parameters, though they remain in the code. The results reported here were calculated after removing these two parameters.

actions in RMAT depend on random events that we could not control, there would have been variation among similar runs. It is important to note that our analysis compares the 257 combinations of parameters against one another with the intent of determining which parameters appear most to influence the values of our chosen outputs. To develop a representative sample of outcomes for each combination of parameters, we performed 50 Monte Carlo trials for each parameter. Our statistical analysis then uses standard approaches to determine which parameters influence the results most.

Our sensitivity testing differs from the way TSA and Boeing use RMAT. Boeing uses RMAT only in forced mode, in which the mode of attack is fixed from the start of each simulation. Boeing runs 425 Monte Carlo cycles for each combination of parameters (for instance, before and after introduction of a countermeasure). Boeing averages the results of the Monte Carlo trials to produce separate baseline and post-countermeasure risk estimates for each output variable. This approach produces expected values of outputs averaged across variations in parameter values and multiple random events that can cause results to take wide swings around their mean values. Thus, whereas the standard Boeing approach is designed to establish stable estimates of what remains most constant across trials, our sensitivity analysis is designed to explore how input values and their different combinations cause outputs to vary away from mean values.

Output parameters. We focused our sensitivity analysis on two model outputs: attack attractiveness and effective number of attacks. Attack attractiveness is the relative merit of an attack from the adversary's perspective.

The effective number of attacks is a measure of damages caused by attacks from the defender's perspective. Effective number of attacks concerns the magnitude of damages produced by an attack, relative to the magnitude of damages the defender might expect if the attack were unmitigated. For example, if the adversary carried out an attack by placing a bomb in checked baggage, but the bomb is intercepted and defused before being loaded onto the airplane, then the effective number of attacks is zero. Alternatively, the bomb may explode but not cause as much damage as planned, allowing the pilot to land the plane safely. In this case, the effective number of attacks will be greater than zero but less than 1.0. It is also possible that the attack causes greater damages than expected, raising the effective number of attacks above 1.0. Similarly, the effective number of attacks can be greater than 1.0 if multiple or parallel attacks are carried out.

We chose these two outputs because of their relevance to TSA analytic needs. Attack attractiveness can be interpreted as the relative likelihood that the adversary will choose one attack over another. The effective number of attacks is a normalized measure of the expected damages caused by a successful, or partially successful, attack.

RMAT configuration. RMAT results are subject to multiple randomized processes, not all of which can be controlled through the interfaces used to edit and vary common parameters. Even when input variables are held constant, therefore, model results will vary. To minimize unwanted sources of variation, all standard deviations of user modifiable input parameters were set to zero. To adjust for the remaining variation in output, we ran each of the 257 excursions through 50 Monte Carlo trials, and averaged the results across the trials.

We conducted the 257 excursions twice—once with RMAT in "competition" mode (Competition Mode Test), where adversaries can choose the most attractive of the available attack options, and once in "forced" mode, where adversaries attempt each available attack option (Forced Mode Test). For each test, we selected five attack options, spanning a range of potential attack effects:

1. Hijack an aircraft and use it as a weapon.
2. Employ a large liquid carry-on bomb.
3. Place a large freight bomb on a passenger aircraft.
4. Place a large bomb on a passenger airplane, is assisted by an insider in the aviation system.
5. Put shooters in the airport lobby.

Analysis. To understand how variations in the 21 input variables influenced the outcomes, we regressed mean outcomes for each NOLH excursion onto the input values using ordinary least squares linear regression. For the Competition Mode Test, where excursions had different numbers of cases for each attack outcome, these regressions were weighted by the frequency of the attack in each excursion.

Results

Of the 257 excursions in our input set, 251 excursions executed properly. A handful of excursions caused RMAT to hang. We did not investigate the cause.

Results for the Competition Mode Test

Despite wide variation in the input values used across trials, the adversary selected one of the five options 95 percent of the time.[4] Attack selection appeared to be determined largely by the expected damage and risk penalty associated with each attack. For example, there is one attack that is usually selected unless the adversary sees a particular detector (such as a canine law enforcement unit), which causes a dramatic reduction in the risk penalty (from 0.93 to less than 0.05), making the attack unattractive. When the detector is encountered, the second most common attack is selected based on the damages it can impart. However, this second attack almost always encounters another detector, again causing a dramatic swing in the risk penalty factor that renders it unattractive.

We found several input variables to have a significant association with each of the outcome variables. Regressions were performed separately for RMAT cases in which each attack option was selected. Interestingly, variations on the 21 parameters selected for this experiment explained a large proportion of the variance for the five attack types and two outcomes, despite the fact that our regression model used a simple linear fit. Indeed, just nine variables could explain between 85 percent and 96 percent of the variance in attractiveness outcomes across each attack type. Similarly, just five variables explained between 46 percent and 96 percent of the variance in effective number of attacks across attack types. This means that despite the interactions and other complexities that RMAT captures, a linear model faithfully describes most

---

[4]   TSA views many of the specific model results as security sensitive information, and therefore they cannot be released in this report. Instead, we offer an overview of the types of findings revealed by the sensitivity analysis.

of the outcome variance. Moreover, it suggests that the variables we selected for analysis are important influences on RMAT outcomes, as we expected.

Many of the significant parameters influence outcomes in the expected direction. For instance, skilled weapon-making predicts effective attacks, and freight detection instrument operator skills predict diminished effective attacks. Nevertheless, there were puzzling associations as well. If the adversary is seeking to maximize economic damage, why would increases in projected economic damages from a freight bomb or insider attacks lead to reductions in their attractiveness? Why does an increasing likelihood of having air marshals onboard make the hijack attack type more attractive?

Several parameters appear to be especially important predictors of attractiveness and effective attacks, for multiple attack types. The sensitivity of model outcomes to these specific parameters is concerning, however, as they are among those we have classed as unverifiable, because little credible information on them can be collected from intelligence or subject matter experts. As such, they are subject to potentially profound imprecision and estimation error. The sensitivity analysis shows that any such imprecision is likely to have a significant effect on model predictions.

Finally, some variables we expected to have an influence on outcomes do not show significant effects. For instance, many observers have suggested that two of the most important air transportation security improvements since 9/11 have been reinforced cockpit doors and vigilant passengers who are prepared to fight back (Goldberg, 2008; Riley, 2011). These parameters do not appear to significantly affect hijack outcomes.[5] None of the parameters tested were significant, and the quality of the statistical model indicates other factors not varied may have been more important.

---

[5] Deterrence is not modeled within RMAT, so the full effect of these security measures may be omitted purposefully.

Results for the Forced Mode Test

Here again, the 21 input variables accounted for a surprising proportion of the variance in outcome results. Seven variables explained between 46 percent and 86 percent of the variance in attractiveness outcomes across attack types; and seven explained between 61 percent and 91 percent of the variance in the effective number of attacks.

Effects are largely in the expected direction. For instance, as the skill of the freight detection instrument operator increases, the attractiveness and success of freight bomb attacks decline. Nevertheless, here too there are some puzzling and unexpected relationships. Why, for instance, would increases in the probability passengers will fight back have a statistically significant and positive effect on the attractiveness of a liquid bomb attack?

There is also a notable omission in the list of significant variables. The probability of successfully entering the flight deck has no significant effect on the attractiveness of hijack attempts or on hijack success rates.

As with the Competition Mode Test results, the variables that appear to have the greatest leverage over model results are those that are also most difficult to estimate with precision.

Summary of Sensitivity Analysis Findings

The analyses carried out using RMAT provide some insight into its operation and behavior. However, because thousands of parameters are related in unknown ways, this analysis is far from comprehensive.

A large proportion of the variance we observe in two outcomes is explained by the linear effects of a small number of input variables. Usually, the relationships between inputs and outputs are in the expected direction, but not always. Moreover, several relationships we expected to find were not present, such as associations between the probability of successfully entering the flight deck and either the attractiveness or success of hijack attempts. We allowed the probability of federal air marshals being present on the hijacked aircraft to vary over a wide range, yet the model suggests that their presence has no significant influence over hijack success rates in forced mode, which is the mode Boeing and TSA currently use.

Of the variables that appear most often to have a significant influence on outcomes, many are those we consider to be difficult or impossible to estimate with precision. These include judgments about how much risk might color the decisions of current and future terrorists or how large the maximum possible size of terrorist cells might be when considering known and unknown groups. Similarly, how large are the teams a terrorist organization would consider fielding? Groups who field no more than one agent per team appear in RMAT to have very different outcomes than those with up to five. How much does the unknown adversary already know about the aviation system before he begins reconnaissance? How efficiently and accurately can the unknown group learn from what they observe? How much direct and indirect damage do terrorists imagine will be produced by each candidate attack?

These are all parameters that are subject to deep uncertainty and, no doubt, to wide variation across terrorist groups. It is not credible that subject matter experts or intelligence can supply useful point estimates of these values. Moreover, even a precisely measured average value would fail to highlight the true nature of risks if some dangerous adversaries have values that are quite different than average. That these variables also happen to explain a large portion of the variance in RMAT outcomes suggests the need for caution when interpreting model results.

In addition to its sensitivity to uncertain parameters, RMAT appears to be highly sensitive to some random processes of the software. For instance, whether an adversary happens to observe a certain detection capability appears to have a dramatic effect on the adversary's judgment about the risks of attempting an insider attack. Whereas RMAT suggests that one particular attack will usually be perceived as essentially risk-free, the rare chance encounter with a specific detector (such as a canine unit) causes the adversary to view the attack as impossibly risky. Again, the sensitivity of model results to somewhat speculative values and causal relationships underscores the importance of interpreting RMAT results with caution.

Verification of Attack Attractiveness

We could not verify the coding of the entire RMAT software but performed a targeted verification by comparing attack attractiveness values logged by the RMAT executable file with those we calculated using input values and the RMAT attractiveness calculation.

We were unable to perform the verification analysis for the competition mode results, because of an RMAT logging error. We consulted with Boeing developers to resolve this inconsistency, but they were unable to explain or repair it during the period of our testing. Boeing provided RAND with a new executable file meant to fix the problems we encountered, but we did not have time to reevaluate it.

We used the same insider attack case to verify the calculation of attractiveness produced by RMAT in the forced mode. Here, we were able to verify that the stated value in the logs is consistent with the functional form. Therefore, the results of this verification indicate that there was a potential problem with either the calculation or the reporting of attractiveness when RMAT was run in competition mode. To date, Boeing has not performed analyses for TSA using the competition mode, so the impact of this error on TSA is negligible. We were not able to determine if the underlying error adversely affects our competition mode sensitivity analyses, though it could.

Configuration Change Management and Testing

Boeing was able to describe and demonstrate many of the processes it uses to manage changes to RMAT. Concurrent Versions System is used to manage the source code. Boeing uses a SharePoint site for recording software errors, data, and model improvements and for documenting that they have been addressed. It also serves as a repository of other documents related to configuration management, testing, and case studies. Boeing uses Microsoft Project for managing the case studies and updating the RMAT code, called "increments" by Boeing. Boeing builds new versions of RMAT as needed, and they are verified by comparing the log files to recent model outputs. Unexpected results as documented in the log files indicate potential errors, which are addressed subsequently. The general process for recording problems and logging their resolution is consistent with standard software maintenance principles.

A greater challenge that appropriate change management processes may not resolve is related to steady evolution of the model without discrete modules that can be independently tested. RMAT uses a "baseline" case that is intended to represent the current state of the adversary and airport security, but the baseline changes frequently in terms of the aviation system configuration, input values, available countermeasures, and attack options. A comparison of two blue agent input files from version 31 and 32 revealed 37 changes: 23 adding, removing, or manipulating agent behavior logic, and 14 that appeared to only change the file's format. A comparison of configuration constant files showed 13 changes: ten related to updating RMAT as a result of an evolving understanding of TSA security such as increasing the level of AIT deployment from 0 to 40 percent, and three comments or deletions. The effects input file also changed. Each such change can produce results that are not directly comparable to results from earlier versions of the baseline. Therefore, it is often not possible to verify that the current version of the model is producing results consistent with previous versions.

The inability to test modules or the entire program for consistency across revisions increases the risk of errors being introduced into the code undetected.

RMAT Software and Management: Satisfaction of Requirements

Table 5.1 summarizes our assessment of agreement in RMAT with four of TSA's risk-assessment requirements concerning usability, performance, and management.

Requirement 16 calls for risk-assessment methods to use and produce data in common file formats. RMAT input and output files are in Extensible Markup Language (XML) and plain text files. The requirement is satisfied.

Table 5.1
RMAT Defender Model Satisfaction of Associated TSA Requirements

Number	Description	RMAT Satisfaction of Requirement
16	Data used and produced by risk assessments should be easy to edit and manipulate.	Yes
17	Risk assessment methods should permit rapid incorporation of new data.	Partial
18	Analysts should be able to modify systme and adversary characteristics.	Yes
22	Risk assessment methods should allow for multiple concurrent studies and quick turnaround risk analyses.	Yes

Requirement 17 requires that risk-assessment methods be kept up to date and sufficiently flexible to allow for rapid updating. Boeing and TSA have established a protocol for incorporating new data into RMAT when necessary to support an analysis. Once data are available, it appears that Boeing is able to incorporate them in a timely fashion to support the analysis. The user input files enable RMAT to be configured quickly when the scope of a study is completely within the boundaries of the current system. However, other tasks are more difficult. For example, adding new agents and the logic governing their behavior requires a developer. Further, the architecture does not easily enable developers to modify logic that is not contained in the user input files. The requirement is partially satisfied.

Requirement 18 concerns the ease with which adversary and aviation system characteristics can be updated by the analyst. As RMAT is currently employed, Boeing is the user of the system. Our experience with RMAT is that the user has the ability to vary the parameters defining the adversary. The requirement is satisfied.

Requirement 22 requires that risk-assessment methods provide sufficient analytic agility to permit multiple simultaneous risk analyses and quick turnaround analyses that provide results within 14 days of problem formulation. Clearly, RMAT and the process supporting it is capable of running multiple risk analyses concurrently. Quick turnaround studies are more difficult, however, because of the detailed data that must be collected and vetted to run case studies. Once the data are collected, the analyses can be run in a week or so. However, collecting the data typically takes a month or more. We acknowledge that data collection time frames are longer and only loosely dependent on RMAT, so we judge this requirement as met.

Conclusions and Recommendations

We can make several recommendations from our inspection of the code, the results of the static code analysis, a limited series of sensitivity analysis, and our review of the software change management processes used by Boeing.

The sensitivity of RMAT results to parameters that cannot be precisely estimated suggests the need for caution when interpreting results based on point estimates for those parameters. Our sensitivity analyses revealed that RMAT results are highly sensitive to multiple parameters that cannot be estimated well. This means that inevitable errors in the estimates used for these parameters can have large effects on model outcomes. Including these sensitivities as part of formal RMAT analyses would help to put the uncertainty of the results in context.

To improve error detection, change management, and model reliability and validity, TSA should consider having Boeing redo the RMAT architecture. The inspection of the code and the results of the static code analysis indicate that RMAT is an example of a software project that has evolved from a prototype and continues to evolve as new ideas emerge about how best to represent the confusing realm of terrorism risks. Because it was not designed to meet specific up-front requirements and was not designed using software engineering principles appropriate for a tool that would be relied on for high-stakes management decisions, RMAT currently suffers from code quality issues related to complexity and module size. Boeing is already addressing some of these issues.

If TSA intends to deploy RMAT as the formal tool for performing aviation risk assessments, then a more streamlined and manageable organization to the code is needed. This would make testing and maintenance of RMAT easier for Boeing and the specification and running of scenarios simpler for TSA. Moreover, the process of developing RMAT through a formal requirements process would ensure that the resulting product has the needed functionality and is able to support the risk-management process at TSA. However, we understand that this may not be realistic given the way RMAT was developed and is used as a supporting part of a larger process. As a tool for promoting thought and development of risk-management strategies, RMAT can continue to add value to the risk-management process in its current form.

If the RMAT architecture is redesigned, special care should be given to working with parameters with unknown (and perhaps unknowable) values. Our sensitivity analyses revealed that model results are highly sensitive to many variables that may be difficult or impossible to estimate. The current design of RMAT treats these parameters as essentially knowable, though often subject to some measurement error. This may not be a good assumption for many of these variables. To the extent that variables that cannot be credibly estimated should be used to represent important phenomena, RMAT and its analytic process should be redesigned to highlight the effects of important uncertainties on model outcomes and to help users understand how their values affect model results. We do not view it as sufficient to allow variation in uncertain parameters but to then treat the average result across these variations as RMAT best estimates of the outcome.

TSA and Boeing should investigate some of the anomalous relationships RAND observed in the sensitivity analysis. We identified several relationships between input variables and model outcomes that we could not explain. These included significant associations in the wrong direction (e.g., increased economic consequences predicting lower success rates and increasing probabilities of air marshals' presence leading to increased hijack attractiveness) and the absence of associations where we would expect to find strong relationships (e.g., the absence of flight deck and federal air marshals' effects on hijack success and attractiveness).

TSA should understand that RMAT is a complex piece of software that is likely to include bugs and errors in addition to those we identified during our review. We identified several software bugs while working with RMAT and reported them to Boeing. Because we were working with the executable file and did not have direct access to the software code, we were unable to trace the sources of the bugs or determine if, for instance, they affected internal calculations of risk or merely concerned how data were logged. Possible errors in the calculation of attractiveness or its logging could make the Competition Mode sensitivity analysis reported in this chapter invalid. Further, the sensitivity analysis covered only 97.5 percent of the test space because of a problem where RMAT would run indefinitely.

Boeing reports being aware of most or all of these bugs and has repaired them. Nevertheless, the difficulties posed by RMAT architecture for maintaining, revising, and debugging the code make it likely that there are or will be additional bugs that could affect model results.

CHAPTER SIX

Supporting TSA Management and Investment Decisions with RMAT

TSA must make high-stakes resource allocation decisions designed to counter threats that are not well known, that are continuously evolving and innovating, and that may intelligently adapt to, evade, or overcome our security measures. If TSA invests in a detection device or imposes a new carry-on restriction, how likely are these countermeasures to reduce overall risk? How should TSA compare countermeasures that affect different risks or that reduce risk to one part of the air transportation system while increasing it elsewhere? Because the risks posed by these threats are shifting and complex, TSA leadership needs analytic tools for understanding the possible implications of policy choices.

RMAT was developed, in part, to support these decisions with valid information about air transportation system risk and the risk reductions that might be expected from existing or planned countermeasures and to do so in ways acceptable to oversight and stakeholder organizations. Accordingly, the tool and supporting processes are being used to evaluate the cost-benefits of AIT, shoe scanners, the SPOT program, and other TSA programs, although in each of these cases, the analyses using RMAT data were developed after major program decisions had already been made. Moreover, TSA would like to use RMAT as part of its answer to such oversight organizations as GAO and DHS that have asked for a structured risk-assessment methodology (e.g., GAO, 2009).

In this chapter, we describe some key features of models that make them useful for decision support and then evaluate RMAT against those features. We conclude with suggestions for improving the use of RMAT for such decisions.

Before proceeding, let us emphasize that what follows is not criticism of RMAT itself. RMAT is an impressive achievement, one that has made real strides in characterizing the terrorist threat to aviation at sufficient levels of detail to allow us to understand the related system problems in ways that were not possible previously. It is a valuable repository of knowledge about a problem that cannot be evaluated except through modeling and simulation. Instead, this chapter is about TSA risk analysis. We believe that RMAT can play a valuable role in TSA analysis but that TSA needs additional tools to supplement RMAT strengths. Further, we believe that some, though definitely not all, of the hopes TSA has had for RMAT are misplaced: high-resolution models are superb for some things and very poor for others.

Therefore, in this chapter, we consider how TSA should or should not use RMAT to serve its risk-assessment needs. This requires some discussion of the risk-assessment processes that RMAT supports, though we emphasize we have not conducted a comprehensive assessment of TSA's risk-assessment processes. Therefore, we limit our discussion to those processes we observed that draw on RMAT results to support policy analysis.

Modeling and Simulation for Decision Support

Major acquisitions, strategic planning, and most resource allocation problems require that decisionmakers anticipate likely future conditions and how different policies or investments will perform under those conditions. If predicting the future were easy or just a matter of plugging the right starting values into a well-constructed model, planning would be easy. But even when current information is very good, such as the data we have on financial markets, our success in predicting the future is spotty at best, and models attempting to forecast the future are often subject to profound and structural sources of uncertainty that can bias predictions in unanticipated ways. This may be especially true when models are designed to predict the behavior of small groups of terrorists, some of whom we know little or nothing about today; whose motivations, intentions, capabilities, and organizations are evolving; and who are studying our defenses to design innovative attacks that circumvent our security.

As noted in TSA's risk-management doctrine (TSA, 2009b), uncertainties about future terrorism, as with uncertainties about future stock market conditions, favor decisions to adopt portfolios of measures that offer robust performance across diverse possible futures, rather than selecting investments that optimize performance but only for a particular set of future conditions.

In the language of decision theory, policymakers should seek strategies that are flexible, adaptive, and robust (FAR strategies; Davis, 2002) to hedge against major uncertainties about the future. Flexible strategies are those that can simultaneously address multiple requirements or objectives, including some that were not anticipated; adaptive strategies anticipate and build in approaches for modifying or changing their approach in response to new information or conditions; and robust strategies perform well across a wide range of possible future conditions.

Modern decision support tools help decisionmakers understand how their options are likely to perform across a range or spanning set of scenarios selected to highlight how deep uncertainties in our current understanding of the future could affect which decisions are best. Deep uncertainties differ importantly from statistical uncertainties that can be estimated when well understood phenomena are subject to uncertainties with probability distributions known through repeated observations. Deep uncertainties exist where we lack vital information about the phenomena under investigation, the mechanisms that produce those phenomena, how parameters interact with each other, and the true values of those parameters or their distributions (Davis, Kulick, and Egner, 2005).

Examples of decision support methods designed to address the effects of deep uncertainty on investments, policy, or strategy include scenario planning (Schwartz, 1996), alternative futures analysis (Slaughter, 2005), capabilities-based planning, portfolio analysis, assumptions-based planning, robust adaptive planning, and robust decisionmaking (Davis, 2002; Davis, Shaver, and Beck, 2008; Dewar et al., 1993; Lempert, Popper, and Bankes, 2003; Groves and Lempert, 2007). Each of these methods seeks in different ways to understand the full range of possible futures, how they relate to multiple objectives, and the policies or investments that offer the most robust benefits across objectives and divergent futures.

Understanding and Communicating RMAT Methods and Assumptions

Complex models such as RMAT present a special challenge to analysts who wish to provide useful and understandable decision support to policymakers. Because these models cannot be validated by comparing their results to a large body of empirical evidence, policymakers will form their own judgments of a model's credibility based in part on its face validity, its intelligibility, the reasoning embodied in the model-based analysis, and their understanding of the scope and applicability of the model.

Indeed, best practices for analytic products generally, and policy analysis modeling specifically, emphasize the importance of transparency and comprehensibility of the model; clear and candid accounting of its caveats, assumptions, and hypotheses; and a thorough assessment of how uncertainties in the model's logic, underlying theory or input data could affect its findings (Bigelow and Davis, 2003; Office of the Director of National Intelligence, 2007; National Research Council, 2008, 2010).

This is a best practice that becomes unwieldy for most high-resolution models such as RMAT that incorporate dozens or hundreds of interacting assumptions and caveats relating to how terrorists think and learn; their objectives and preferences; their resources, skills, and capabilities; and the types of attacks they might consider. In the case of RMAT, for instance, consider just the caveating required to explain current design choices for what counts as part of the modeled air transportation system. A partial listing of caveats just for defining the scope of the system would include the following:

- RMAT models domestic, commercial air transportation of freight and passengers but not other transportation modes or commercial aviation associated with the general aviation system.
- RMAT models risk to domestic air travel but not the risk from inbound foreign commercial transportation to the domestic system, such as those posed by the shoe-bomber, Richard Reid; the Christmas Day bomber, Umar Farouk Abdulmutallab; or the al-Qa'ida in the Arabian Peninsula printer cartridge bombs.
- RMAT primarily models security measures performed at the airport or in planes but not most law enforcement activities that occur outside the airport, such as those leading to the arrests in Britain of terrorists planning a liquid bomb attack on commercial flights.
- RMAT does not consider air transportation system vulnerabilities that involve information or communication systems, such as booking systems, air traffic control systems, or navigation systems.
- RMAT considers only the risk associated with 67 prespecified attack options, including most system vulnerabilities included in the TSSRA air transportation system risk models other than chemical and biological attacks.
- RMAT describes the current configuration of airport security, which is limiting for analyses designed to describe risk beyond the next major successful attack that results in major changes to airport operations or security.
- RMAT assumes that all airports are essentially equivalent in terms of vulnerabilities and security operations. Thus, for instance, Reagan National Airport in the Washington, D.C., metro area is exposed to no different risks or vulnerabilities than Cincinnati/ Northern Kentucky International Airport.
- RMAT does not attempt to describe the absolute risks to the system, rather just the relative risks, or changes in magnitude of risk, associated with modifications to the system, assuming that for any growth or decline in absolute risk, countermeasures can be assumed to have proportional growth or decline in their risk-reducing effects.

Each of these caveats, and many others concerning the types of terrorists modeled, how risks are defined, the types of attack consequences modeled, and other design characteristics has important but often murky implications for how to interpret model results. It is true that RMAT could be further developed to eliminate some or all of these caveats, but it is unlikely that such improvements would succeed in eliminating many major caveats.

RMAT is designed to highlight how attackers might adapt to or circumvent security measures. For instance, if it becomes too difficult to smuggle a weapon through the passenger checkpoint, RMAT might suggest that the attacker will pursue the same attack using an insider to convey weapons to the sterile area of the airport. As such, the model is properly described as one that captures the risk-shifting that TSA recognizes as a principal characteristic of the intelligent adversaries it must counter.

In recent practice, however, RMAT is run in forced mode, in which attackers are not allowed to respond adaptively to security measures by shifting to an alternative attack. Forced mode is used in lieu of competition mode, where attackers select the most attractive attack from a set of alternatives. Forced mode is preferred because it reduces reliance on some of the uncertain assumptions in the adversary model about target selection, and because comparison of the attractiveness of each attack before and after introduction of a countermeasure can provide a more refined understanding of where risk might be shifting, and why.

Results from RMAT when it is run in forced mode provide conditional estimates of risk. That is, they provide estimates of the likelihood of success or consequences *conditional on an attack of that type being attempted*. The advantage of considering conditional risks and risk reductions is that they provide program managers with a clear understanding of how a specific countermeasure affects the risk of attacks such as those it was designed to counter. For instance, the 3-1-1 policy was designed to prevent liquid explosives from entering the system through checkpoints. By examining change in conditional risk before and after adoption of the policy, we can provide an estimate of the number of liquid explosives attacks that were prevented, assuming that there is no adaptation in the means of bringing liquid explosives onto planes. This type of analysis can be useful for evaluating the effectiveness of a technology or policy for a given narrow objective, but it is less useful for evaluating the cost-benefits of the new technology. To establish cost-benefits, we should be more interested in understanding how introduction of the countermeasure reduces overall system risk, not just the risk of a particular, narrow attack type.

Conditional risks also may be especially difficult to interpret and communicate clearly to policymakers. For instance, consider using this approach to evaluate the effects of a new countermeasure, such as a new passenger screening technology at the checkpoint. Figure 6.1 illustrates what such an analysis might look like for four attack strategies. The new checkpoint technology appears to reduce expected losses conditional on either a body bomb or hijack attempt but has no effect on insider and freight attack vectors.

Because each of the risk-reduction estimates is conditional on a different event, the risk and risk-reduction estimates in Figure 6.1 are not strictly comparable. That is, the large body bomb risk reduction is

Figure 6.1
Expected Losses per Attack for Four Types of Attack

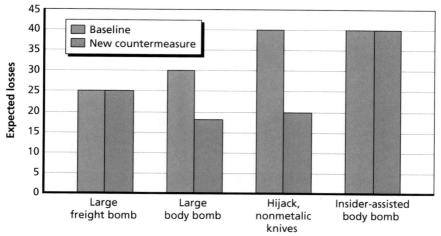

NOTE: The data in the figure are fabricated and are for illustration only.
RAND *MG1241-6.1*

conditional on a large body bomb attack being attempted, whereas the hijack risk reduction is conditioned on that type of attack. By using RMAT in forced choice mode, results such as those depicted in Figure 6.1 no longer conform to the familiar conceptualization of risk as

$$Risk_i = P(Attack_i \ occurs) * P(Attack_i \ Succeeds) * Consequence(Attack_i),$$

for all attack types, i. Instead, risks in Figure 6.1 can be formulated as

$$Risk_{i|i} = P(Attack_i \ Succeeds | Attack_i \ Occurs) * Consequence(Attack_i),$$

where $Risk_{i|i}$ is the risk attributable to attacks of type i, conditional on attempts of that type. To render the different conditional risk estimates comparable, they must be multiplied by the probability of the attack occurring:

$$Risk_i = P(Attack_i \ Succeeds | Attack_i \ Occurs) * \\ Consequence(Attack_i) * P(Attack_i \ occurs).$$

In other words, the baseline and countermeasure risk estimates in Figure 6.1 are misleading until they have been multiplied by the probability that each attack type occurs. For instance, if the probability of occurrence of freight bombs, body bombs, hijack, and insider attacks were 0.1, 0.08, 0.05, and 0.01, respectively, it would be wrong to conclude from Figure 6.1 that hijack and insider represent the greatest baseline threats. In fact, they would be the lowest. And it would be wrong to conclude that the new technology offers greater risk reduction for hijack than for body bomb. The reverse would be true.

Borrowing an example used by Mueller and Stewart (2011), the conditional risk of a tsunami in Columbus, Ohio, might be very large, and no doubt it would be larger than the conditional risk of, say, a large conventional bomb. Moreover, the risk reduction that could be achieved by building a network of strong sea walls might be considerable. It is not until the probability of the tsunami in Columbus is factored into these risk estimates that a meaningful comparison of tsunami and conventional bomb attacks can be made, at which point the apparently greater tsunami risk can be seen to be trivial by comparison to that of the explosive.

In cases where the probability of attack changes from one attack type to another, or from baseline to after introduction of a counter-measure, these conditional values are not comparable, so should not be used to estimate relative risk. For example, it is easy to imagine a case where introduction of a countermeasure increases the cost and time required for the adversary to mount an attack, but conditional on the attack being attempted the probability of success is the same as it was before introduction of the countermeasure. Using the current approach to understanding risk reduction, one would falsely conclude that the countermeasure offers no risk reduction. However, if the probability of attack is diminished by the increased adversary time and costs, the true effect of the countermeasure is to reduce risk. Similar examples result in the current procedure overestimating risk reduction.

Even when data such as those in Figure 6.1 are produced by run-ning RMAT in competition mode, there are problems with using such data to extrapolate likely cost benefits. If the cost of the new technology is just $10 million, a policymaker might view this chart and conclude that the $12 million or $20 million reduction in expected losses after the first body bomb or hijack attempt would more than pay for the new technology. That would be correct, but making the benefits con-ditional on adversaries continuing to pursue these forms of attack after introduction of the new technology requires doubtful assumptions that violate TSA's risk-management doctrine (TSA, 2009b). In particular, it assumes that adversaries will not adapt to the countermeasure by pursuing a different attack strategy. In this illustrative example, for instance, a rational adversary might respond to the new countermea-sure by instead pursuing a freight bomb attack. In that case, the benefit of the new technology is more like $5 million for the first attack, rather than the $12 million the policymaker assumed. Or the attacker might be pushed to pursue the insider-assisted body bomb attack, in which-case the new technology would not only cost $10 million but could encourage greater losses than would otherwise be expected.[1]

Moreover, it may be that attackers are not chiefly focused on smuggling weapons through the checkpoint. In Figure 6.1, for instance, attackers seeking to maximize expected losses might be more interested in an insider-assisted body-bomb attack, in which case the new technology offers no benefits.

In each example, the apparent benefit of the technology depends on the assumptions that terrorists are considering only attacks that require smuggling weapons through the checkpoint and that they will not respond adaptively to new technologies by seeking alternative attack strategies. There is an extensive literature demonstrating the weakness of these assumptions (Jackson et al., 2007), and TSA's risk-management doctrine emphasizes the need to account for terrorist adaptation and the risk-displacement effects of new countermeasures.

A related concern is that defenders too are adaptive. When attackers succeed or even come close, the United States is likely to respond as it has in the past with new security procedures and technologies. The pictures RMAT can paint with graphs such as Figure 6.1 represent an estimate of current risk, but it may be a poor depiction of risk after the next attack. This is particularly important to convey to decisionmakers, since it has implications for how they understand the risk-reduction benefits of a new technology. Indeed, it raises questions about whether RMAT in its present form can satisfy Requirement 2, which states that risk-reduction estimates should be calculated for a 5–10 year acquisition planning horizon, taking into account the evolution of defender systems.

For instance, suppose the new technology described in Figure 6.1 costs $50 million. The policymaker might be inclined to believe that the benefits of the new technology will outweigh its costs after just

---

[1] The analysis here assumes that terrorists can shift between alternative attack modes freely. In fact, some alternative modes may be difficult to plan and prepare for, in which case the countermeasure forcing such adaptation should get more risk-reduction credit than we are suggesting. Understanding time lines for adapting to countermeasures represents an interesting, and potentially important, feature of terrorism risk estimation that has not yet been undertaken.

a few body-bomb or hijack attempts. Almost certainly, this inference would be incorrect. History suggests transportation security will evolve in response to any serious attempts, whether or not they are successful, with the likely effect of changing the risk-reduction benefits of existing programs:

- After the Pan Am bombing over Lockerbie, laptops and other electronic devices such as those suspected of housing the bomb became subject to routine scrutiny, likely reducing the effectiveness other checkpoint processes such as carry-on luggage screening and explosive trace detection.
- After the attempted shoe-bombing by Richard Reid, shoes were subjected to X-ray screening, potentially affecting the performance of carryon luggage screening and explosive trace detection.
- After the London liquid bombers were disrupted, new liquid restrictions were put in place, which not only complicated checkpoint baggage screening but might also have modified the effectiveness of luggage screening and explosive trace detection technology.
- After the 2009 Christmas Day body-bomb attempt, full-body scanners and enhanced patdown procedures were implemented, reducing the benefits attributable to magnetometers.

It is likely, therefore, that after the next attempted or successful attack, security measures will be implemented that alter the current risk benefits that RMAT calculates for a countermeasure. Thus, cost-benefit calculations that assume an accumulation of benefits using current-day RMAT estimates are likely to overestimate the benefits of the technology. Instead, it would be reasonable to assume that security benefits degrade over time as the system and attacker capabilities evolve.

Risk Assessment for Decision Support: Satisfaction of Requirements

Six high-priority risk-assessment requirements concern either how risk is modeled or how risk results can be used. On the basis of the discussion above, we evaluate that RMAT alone cannot satisfy most of these requirements, though it can often partially satisfy them subject to important caveats.

Requirement 1 calls for conceptualizations of risk to be consistent with TSA risk principles. This is a challenge, because TSA's risk-management doctrine offers a sophisticated understanding of the complexities of terrorism risk management (TSA, 2009b). In particular, it emphasizes the following points:

- *Terrorists are adaptive, so countermeasures may cause attack strategies or targets to shift.* As noted above, RMAT is designed to allow for such risk-shifting, at least among predefined attack types. However, this competition mode in which terrorists can choose the most attractive available option is not currently used by TSA, and the probabilities of success estimates drawn from RMAT in this mode do not properly account for risk-shifting. Instead, estimates of attack attractiveness, probabilities of success, and expected damages are estimated conditionally, depending on which type of attack is selected. This approach can still offer insights into terrorist adaptation and resulting risk-shifting. But the estimates of pre- and post-countermeasure risk for any particular attack do not account for risk-shifting when results are produced in forced mode. Instead, the user must examine how risk appears to have shifted for other attacks after introduction of the countermeasure, though insights from these comparisons are quite general, rather than quantitative, because as discussed above, risk reductions for different attacks should not be treated as occurring on equivalent scales. Therefore, when TSA analysts present their leadership with RMAT results, they routinely caveat the results with a warning that risk-shifting is not accounted for. TSA reports that it has taken steps to develop a methodology to better account for deterrence and threat-shifting, but we did not review this method.

- *A key benefit of security may be deterrence.*[2] As it is currently used, RMAT assumes that attackers will mount an attack. This means that RMAT attackers proceed with an attack even when they stand no reasonable chance of success. As discussed in Chapter Two, this is a poor assumption, as many terrorists have proven to be highly risk-averse. If none of the available attacks stands an acceptable chance to succeed, terrorists are likely to be deterred from them, to shift their attacks outside the air transportation system, or to adopt a new attack strategy other than those anticipated by RMAT. RMAT is not currently designed to account for these outcomes, so TSA risk analysts advise their leadership to adjust their understanding of RMAT results to account for deterrence effects.

- *Terrorism risks often involve unanticipated attacks.* Terrorists can be expected to study our security defenses and to plan attacks that our security systems do not adequately anticipate and counter. Moreover, because we lack key information about terrorist capabilities and intentions, which may be evolving continuously, we lack critical information about the types of attacks to expect. Because RMAT evaluates risk on a predefined set of attack strategies and makes no allowance for a background level of risk that cannot be further reduced, RMAT requires the implicit assumption that there will be no surprises—an assumption inconsistent with TSA risk doctrine. A simple adjustment that could address this concern would be to add one more attack type to those modeled, called "some other attack." By setting the presumed attrac-

---

[2] Here, Requirement 1 is not entirely consistent with Requirement 7, which states that modeling deterrence effects is a low priority. We disagree with this rating and agree with the emphasis that the TSA risk doctrine places on deterrence effects. If there is a probability of success below which attackers are not willing to risk their efforts, countermeasures designed to further reduce attacker success will incorrectly appear in RMAT to effectively reduce system risk. Since there is good evidence that attackers may require very high levels of success to proceed (e.g., Enders and Sandler, 2002), the omission of such deterrence effects could dramatically bias estimates of the relative risk reductions attributable to new security systems.

tiveness of this background or unexpected risk option to a range of levels, it may be possible to get a truer understanding of the likely risk-reduction benefits associated with countermeasures directed against those attacks we can anticipate.

- *TSA and other security providers must continuously adapt and innovate to address emerging risks.* TSA correctly views risk management as a dynamic process that evolves continuously. RMAT is not designed to anticipate this evolution. Instead, it is designed to offer a view of current risk and how it might be affected by new countermeasures. As discussed above, extrapolations of such risk estimates to the future, especially any future that follows another attempted attack or the introduction of a new security system, are almost certainly unwarranted. For this reason, TSA needs other tools or processes for considering how risk-reduction estimates suggested by RMAT may be likely to degrade over time to derive estimates that satisfy Requirement 2, which states that risk analyses should provide risk-reduction estimates for a 5–10 year planning horizon.

- *Because future terrorism risks are subject to sources of deep uncertainty, TSA does not seek to minimize point estimates of future risk but rather seeks to identify risk-mitigation solutions that counter a wide spectrum of possible future risks.* TSA decisionmakers need information on the risk reductions that will be produced by new security measures. Since we are poor at predicting the future, decision theory used at the Department of Defense and elsewhere emphasizes identifying options that are robust to deep uncertainties in such prediction exercises. In practice, this typically means using exploratory analysis to evaluate decision outcomes across a set of test cases selected to span all key sources of deep uncertainty (Davis, Shaver, and Beck, 2008). TSA uses sensitivity analysis methods that can span a portion of the uncertain future. That is, as it is currently used, RMAT calculates an estimate of current or baseline risk from which risk reductions are calculated for new security measures under a set of excursions from a best estimate of the measure's risk-reduction effects. These excursions explore assumptions concerning the expected number of attacks per year, whether the attacker has low or high capabilities, several deployment options, and expected technology improvements. This approach provides insights into the robustness of the RMAT results to the tested assumptions, but these analyses depend strongly on the validity of the base case assumptions and many other uncertain variables that are not systematically explored. In reality, the baseline is not at all like a good "best estimate" around which to do excursions.[3] This approach does not explore the entire space of plausible futures, nor does it clarify which RMAT assumptions may be most important for determining outcomes.

TSA has also piloted a "capability gaps" process, partially modeled on DoD's capability development model, which is intended to find security solutions that are robust across a range of risks. TSA uses RMAT results as one of several risk and intelligence inputs into the process. However, TSA has yet to fully formalized this process, and we did not review it as part of this study.

RMAT can be used to study how particular sources of deep uncertainty affect results, but it is not designed to support a comprehensive assessment of how major sources of uncertainty, understood at a higher level of abstraction, affect risk assessments. Thus, we conclude that RMAT does not satisfy Requirement 5, which requires that the tool provide accurate information on any uncertainty in model results.

Because RMAT does not or only partially satisfies these core TSA risk-management principles, we conclude that RMAT only partially satisfies Requirement 1.

---

[3] By this we mean that, although the baseline may be as reasonable a single case as any other, it is no more likely than some very different cases. Thus, sensitivity analysis around the baseline, for a given parameter, may greatly understate the actual sensitivity because, with an equally plausible baseline, sensitivity would be much higher. This was a core motivation in the development of exploratory analysis in DoD work (see Davis, 2002, and the references therein to work tracing back to the 1980s). See also a white paper developed for DoD's master plan for modeling and simulation (Davis and Henninger, 2007, p. xii, which also lists recommended functional requirements for models).

Requirement 4 requires risk assessments that estimate absolute and relative risk and risk reduction. Although RMAT produces estimates of expected losses per attack attempt, it was never intended to estimate the likelihood of attempts, so it cannot estimate absolute levels of risk. As such, whereas RMAT can partially meet this TSA need, TSA will need to rely on other tools or methods to produce absolute risk estimates, such as the Transportation Sector Security Risk Assessment, which is designed to provide absolute risk estimates. TSA reports that it is currently working on a process to better integrate TSSRA results into its risk-modeling and analytic products.

In lieu of absolute risk estimates, RMAT calculates relative risk reductions conditional on attacks. RMAT developers emphasize that because the absolute risk of any attack is not estimated for the model, the conditional risk is not itself meaningful. Instead, the more meaningful risk measure is relative risk-reduction calculated for any changes from baseline conditional risk. That is, for any set of security measures, RMAT results seek to describe the proportion of baseline risk each countermeasure could be expected to eliminate and to do so in a way that allows the relative benefits of each countermeasure to be compared. That is, RMAT calculates risk reduction, RR_i, for each countermeasure, i, as

$$RR_i = \frac{BR - CR_i}{BR},$$

where BR is system risk at baseline, and CR_i is risk after introduction of countermeasure i.

Relative risk estimates such as these are used to estimate the benefits of new countermeasures without necessarily knowing the true level of baseline risk. In doing so, however, they make strong assumptions about features of absolute risk that are unlikely to be correct. For instance, unless we can assume that CR_i scales with BR, for all countermeasures (that is, that $CR_i = BR*a$, for some constant. a), it is clear from the equation above that RR is not a value that is independent of absolute risk and will yield different estimates of the value of countermeasures depending on that absolute risk level.

The assumption that CR scales linearly with BR is a poor assumption, since few countermeasures will affect all sources of system risk uniformly. That is, suppose baseline risk is made up of several discrete components of system risk, for example, risks associated with the checkpoint, C, risks associated with cargo, A, and risks associated with insiders, I, so that $BR = C + A + I$. Then, any countermeasure that affects only one of those component sources of system risk, say, reducing insider risk by d, would result in $CR = C + A + (I - d)$. For it to be true that $CR = BR^*a$, then

$$C + A + I - d = a(C + A + I), \text{ or } d = (1 - a)BR,$$

meaning that the benefits of security improvements to any component of system risk must also scale with total system risk. This leads to the perplexing conclusion that if the true risk to which the passenger checkpoint is exposed doubles, but the risks associated with cargo and insiders is unchanged, the risk benefits associated with our insider countermeasure must nevertheless be assumed to increase.

As RMAT results are currently used to support cost-effectiveness estimates, an additional problem with RMAT risk estimates should be addressed in TSA's risk assessment process. TSA does not use RMAT estimates of expected defender consequences of attacks, favoring, instead, estimates of attack consequences generated by another TSA risk-assessment process, the Transportation Sector Security Risk Assessment (TSA, 2010), so that a consistent set of consequence estimates are used across TSA analytic products. Thus, TSA calculates independent estimates of expected losses, by multiplying the RMAT probabilities of success for individual attacks by TSSRA estimates of the likely consequences of those attacks. This approach is attractive because it uses more comprehensive consequence data than what are available in RMAT, though the TSSRA estimates suffer many of the limitations we note in Chapter Three for the RMAT cost estimates. However, RMAT probabilities of successful attack result from the adversary's selecting weapon-target pairings based on a different set of consequence estimates than TSA is using to extrapolate expected consequences. It is possible that the adversary would select different attacks or different numbers of parallel attacks and achieve different probabilities of success if TSSRA consequence estimates instead of RMAT consequence estimates were used in the adversary's calculation of attack attractiveness.

A further limitation to the RMAT risk estimates was discussed in Chapter Four. Specifically, risk is meaningfully described only over some definite time period. Expected losses of $1 million over a year would represent twice as much risk as the same losses over two years. However, RMAT relative risks are not defined for a specific time period. This is partially because RMAT time steps are not calibrated to represent time accurately. In addition, however, even if the times associated with events in RMAT were well calibrated, RMAT runs until an attack occurs or until ten simulation years expire. Each attack could take less than a year, or more than a year, but the simulation for the trial ends with the attack. If 200 trials lead to 100 successful attacks, that corresponds to a 50 percent chance of successful attack over multiple different time frames. It would not be correct to say it is a 50 percent chance of success over a ten-year time frame, since presumably risk does not drop to 0 after an attack attempt as is implied when RMAT ends each trial after an attempt.

In short, RMAT does not produce estimates of absolute risk. Its estimates of relative risk reductions are subject to strong, probably untenable assumptions. Finally, RMAT risks are not defined for a coherent time period. For these reasons, we conclude that RMAT cannot satisfy TSA's risk-assessment Requirement 4.

Requirements 20 and 21 call for risk assessments that can be used to support policy and acquisition decisions and for communications with GAO and other oversight and stakeholder groups. We believe that RMAT could be more effectively used in support of other risk-assessment tools that might be shared with policymakers, an idea we develop in the next section. As such, we rate Requirement 20 as partially met with RMAT.

Whether RMAT satisfies GAO, NIPP, or other risk-management requirements is less clear, in part because the minimum requirements for meeting the standards of risk assessment for these organizations are not well defined. GAO (2009) has emphasized that TSA needs a way to systematically integrate threat, vulnerability, and consequence information in a way that stands up to independent validation. Similarly, the National Research Council (NRC, 2008, 2010) has argued that DHS needs risk tools that are transparent, easily communicated, well documented, and which have been reviewed satisfactorily through journal peer review processes or other rigorous standards of independent validation.

Clearly, RMAT represents an attempt to address GAO concerns by systematically integrating threat, vulnerability, and consequence information. Similarly, TSA's interest in requesting an independent assessment of the model's validity takes a step in the direction proposed by GAO and the National Academy.

Models not subject to validation through comparison with a large body of empirical evidence may not be valid for prediction but can be very useful for helping analysts and decisionmakers explore the nature of the phenomena that must be understood and for exploring possible implications of alternative assumptions and input values. To serve in such an explanatory role, analyses depend very much on transparent and valid conceptual models that can be clearly and persuasively communicated. RMAT is a highly complex model subject to dozens of deep uncertainties, major caveats, and assumptions, all of which make easy communication with stakeholders and oversight groups difficult.

Despite these limitations, we recognize, and we expect that DHS and GAO will recognize, that RMAT represents a significant step forward in structuring what all agree is a very difficult and unsolved problem in a way designed to lead to more reliable risk estimates. For this reason, we consider that RMAT partially meets TSA's requirement for risk assessments that will meet the expectations of oversight organizations (Requirement 21).

Recommendations: Improving the Use of RMAT and the Interpretation of Its Results

To meet some of TSA's principal intended uses, it should develop an exploratory and multiresolution modeling framework in which RMAT could be incorporated. Bigelow and Davis (2003) note that with predictive models, analysts typically establish a base case, then test how the future is likely to change under a small number of modifications to the base case. Whether explicitly or implicitly, this approach treats model outputs as reasonable guesses as to how the world would look if it is properly described by the model's input conditions.

In general, predictive models are appropriate when the theory guiding the model's design is well developed and accepted, where the typical variation between model predictions and reality can be established over multiple trials, and where the data used by the model are valid and reliable, except, perhaps, for a small number of variables for which sensitivity analysis can be used to highlight their possible implications for model results (Dewar et al., 1996).

Where models are subject to deep uncertainties about the mechanisms producing modeled outcomes or parameter values, *exploratory analysis* is more appropriate (Davis, 2002; Davis, Shaver, and Beck, 2008). With exploratory analysis, base cases are usually irrelevant. Instead, the objective is to systematically look across the space of possibilities created by varying parameter values simultaneously to understand not an average expected outcome but rather the input conditions under which the model produces qualitatively different outcomes.

As the number of uncertain parameters grows, the number of possible combinations of input values explodes, so as a practical matter, exploratory analysis becomes infeasible or at least dubious with more than 10 or 12 uncertain parameters. The problem is not primarily the computational burden of the combinatorial explosion of cases but rather analysts' and decisionmakers' inability to comprehend, reason, and communicate coherently and persuasively about results that might involve interactions among a great many variables. Decisionmakers need to be able to understand the high-level tradeoffs that are most important to the outcomes that they are responsible for. A multivariate solution with many dozens of tradeoffs cannot be formulated into a useful and communicable narrative that explains how decisions were arrived at.

In current practice, RMAT has been used to explore characteristics of aviation system risk such as risk-shifting, to examine the sensitivity of risk-reduction estimates to some sources of deep uncertainty such as adversary capabilities, and it has been used as a predictive model when, for instance, RMAT results are used as benefit estimates for cost benefit analysis. When RMAT is used as a predictive model, TSA has been careful to explore the effects of some deep uncertainties on modeled benefits, providing insights for decisionmakers about the possible effects of, for instance, adversary skill levels on the risk reductions expected for new countermeasures. However, these methods necessarily condition results on many other assumptions and caveats that are not transparent, and depend on a conceptualization of risk reduction that does not fully account for important insights from TSA's risk doctrine.

A better approach is to develop a multiresolution *family* of models (National Research Council, 1997), some of which may be in the same overall program (with switches to activate or deactivate optional higher-resolution modules) and some of which may be fully separate models but with known relationships and mechanisms for cross-calibration. The different members of such a family will typically have very different strengths and shortcomings, as summarized in a white paper done in support of Department of Defense modeling and simulation planning, drawing on suggestions from community-wide meetings (Davis and Henninger, 2007).

The relatively low-resolution members of such a family are analytically nimble and can be easy to explain and understand; they have far fewer input parameters, which can be subjected to detailed exploratory analysis (Davis, 2003; Bigelow and Davis, 2003; Dewar et al., 1996; Davis, Shaver, and Beck, 2008). Ideally, in such a family, the lower-resolution models are explicit but approximate abstractions of sound higher-resolution models, perhaps with the abstractions chosen for analysis in support of a particular decision. In addition to permitting a detailed exploration of the parameter space and its implications for the pending decision, low-resolution models can improve the transparency and interpretability of the model for the analyst's clients. Moreover, in some cases, low-resolution models can help explain seemingly paradoxical results from higher-resolution models, or, as illustrated by

Bigelow and Davis (2003), they can even be used to identify errors in higher-resolution models.

Where the high-resolution model is solid enough (albeit subject to uncertainties), it can be exercised and analyzed statistically to generate lower-resolution models. RAND analysts have recommended doing so in a theory-informed manner, leading to "motivated meta models" (Bigelow and Davis, 2003) rather than the more common "response surfaces" that do not typically allow for meaningful interpretation. An example of a motivated meta model might be the simple regression models we showed in Chapter Five, which could explain most of RMAT results. The point is not that RMAT could be replaced with such meta models but rather that the metamodels could be used to help decisionmakers understand high-level tradeoffs and explain the rationale of their decisions.

RMAT could be used to support compelling and transparent low-resolution models that could be used for exploratory analysis in ways that improve decisionmakers' intuitions and understanding of choices. To illustrate, we will outline a simplified version of such an approach. The objective of our example is to provide decisionmakers with information useful in deciding whether to invest in a new security program that could reduce the likelihood of one type of attack (Attack C). Specifically, the analysis should clarify the future conditions under which investment in the new security program appears likely to offer significant risk-reduction benefits, after accounting for sources of deep uncertainty.

There are many variables we cannot estimate well with available science or intelligence. Because some of these uncertainties concern, for instance, how future unknown threats might materialize, even subject matter experts do not offer sufficiently credible information that our model results could be treated as offering meaningful information about the performance of our security systems. Instead, the caveats on the deep uncertainties would necessarily be so great as to undermine decisionmaker confidence in the modeled results.

However, the analyst using a low-resolution model built on RMAT and other data sources could provide decisionmakers with a detailed understanding of how deep uncertainties might affect optimal security decisions. Often, at this high level of analysis, the decision problem can be reduced to a small number of key uncertainties. In our simple example, for instance, we have identified three key sources of uncertainty to examine:

- *Indirect economic effects of terrorist attacks.* As we noted in Chapter Three, RMAT estimates of indirect consequences focus exclusively on effects experienced by the air transportation industry. In truth, however, a broader view of the economy is likely to see compensatory growth in other parts of the economy, and the cascading economic effects of both shocks represent a notoriously complex problem (Enders, 2007). Moreover, since the choice of attacks depends on the attackers' perception of the likely indirect effects, even the best available economic models of indirect costs may be poor proxies for attacker judgments of these effects. Therefore, in our illustrative example, we consider a range of possible indirect costs that span more than an order of magnitude (Table 6.1).
- *Attacker capabilities.* Although we have good intelligence on the aspirations and capabilities of some threatening groups, we have

Table 6.1
Risk Modeling Requirements Satisfied by RMAT

Number	Short Description	RMAT Satisfaction of Requirements
1	Risk conceptualization should be consistent with TSA principles.	Partial
2	Risk reduction should be calculated for a 5–10 year planning horizon.	No
4	Risk assessments should provide estimates of absolute and relative risk and risk reduction.	No
5	Risk assessments should provide accurate information on any uncertainty in model results.	No
20	Risk assessments should provide risk information useful for high-priority resource allocation decisions.	Partial
21	Risk assessments should be acceptable to oversight and stakeholder organizations.	Partial

little information on the capabilities they may have in the next few years when our new security system could be deployed. Moreover, there may be other groups or individuals with capabilities we are not yet aware of. For these reasons, attacker capabilities represent another key source of uncertainty that we represent in our model as probabilities of success ranging from incompetence (almost no chance of success) to high competence (Table 6.2).

- *Deterrence.* Homeland security executives know little about the deterrence effects of security systems other than that deterrence effects are vitally important (Morral and Jackson, 2009). Because so little is known, RMAT assumes that no attack can be deterred. That is, RMAT forces attackers to attempt an attack no matter how unlikely it is to succeed. Clearly, deterrence effects represent a key uncertainty for understanding the effects of any new countermeasure. For our illustrative analysis, we consider three levels of deterrence effects: No deterrence effects, medium deterrence effects (attackers are deterred from any attack with 25 percent or lower chance of success), and high deterrence effects (attackers are deterred from any attack with 50 percent or lower chance of success).

For the purposes of this simplified model, we additionally assume that the attacker values each death at $7 million and seeks to maximize expected losses, which can be expressed as the sum of losses from deaths, direct costs, and indirect costs multiplied by the probability of success. Both of these assumptions could also be treated as sources of deep uncertainty, but to simplify this illustrative example, we treat them as known.

Using the data and assumptions described above for our low-resolution model, Table 6.2 (Panel A) shows how the three major sources of uncertainty affect our baseline risk, or what we believe attackers view as the most attractive attacks in the absence of the new technology. Across the parameter space defined by our uncertainty variables, our low-resolution model shows that there are conditions under which all five candidate attacks might be preferred by some attacker, with the lowest-capability attacker preferring the less consequential and easier

Table 6.2
Example Low-Resolution Model of the Effects of Uncertainty on the Risk Reduction Expected from a New Technology (Fabricated Data)

A. Terrorist Baseline Attack Preferences			
		(low/high indirect cost assumptions)	
Deterrence	High		D/D	C/B
	Medium	E/E	C/C	A/B
	None	C/D	C/C	A/B
		Low	Medium	High
		terrorist capabilities (probability of success)		

B. Terrorist Technology Preferences			
		(low/high indirect cost assumptions)	
Deterrence	High		D/D	B/B
	Medium	E/E	B/D	A/B
	None	C/D	A/D	A/B
		Low	Medium	High
		terrorist capabilities (probability of success)		

C. Terrorist Baseline Attack Preference			
		(low/high indirect cost assumptions)	
Deterrence	High	0/0	0/0	96/0
	Medium	0/0	309/30	0/0
	None	352/0	242/30	0/0
		Low	Medium	High
		terrorist capabilities (probability of success)		

NOTES: In panel B, red letters highlight adversary preferences that change as a result of the new security measure. In Panel C, red cells indicate no risk reduction benefits, yellow cells indicate risk reduction benefits only when the adversary judges the indirect consequences of attacks to be low, and green cells indicate risk reduction benefits regardless of adversary judgments about indirect consequences.

attacks, C, D, and E, although if low-capability attackers are subject to high deterrence effects, they would select none of the five attack options. The medium capability attackers prefer attack C if they are impossible or hard to deter, or D if subject to high deterrence effects. The most capable attackers prefer attack B if they judge indirect consequences to be high, or attack A if they are not easily deterred and perceive indirect economic costs to be lower.

Across the baseline parameter space, attack C appears to be the most widely preferred attack. Suppose now that the new security program reduces the probabilities of success with attack C by half for all attacker types (this, too, is probably an assumption we would want to examine in a more complete exploratory analysis). Although the expected consequences of attack C are halved, it would be incorrect to attribute benefits of this magnitude to the new program, since other attacks would likely be substituted by rational terrorists seeking to maximize expected consequences.

Table 6.2 (Panel B) shows attack preferences after introduction of the new security program. As expected, in five of six cases where attack C was preferred at baseline, the effect of the new security program has been to shift preferences to alternative attacks with better expected consequences (we have highlighted these substituted attacks in red in the table).

If we had sought to estimate the reduction in losses attributable to the new security program by taking our best estimates of each uncertainty parameter and then assuming that we could attribute to the program all the reduced losses expected from attacks of type C, we would almost certainly overstate the true benefits of the program. For instance, if our best estimates settled on a high-capability attacker who could not be deterred and who risked causing high indirect costs, we would conclude that the new program offers well over $4 billion in reduced losses per attack of type C.

Our low-resolution model offers a potentially more persuasive assessment of the likely benefits of a countermeasure than would RMAT alone, because it allows inherently unknowable variables to range across values spanning the full uncertainty space and because it allows for risk displacement onto alternative attacks in response to the new security program, and does so with fairly modest and transparent speculation on how attackers might go about making such decisions. Specifically, Table 6.3 (Panel C) shows the reduced losses associated with the change in attack preferences from baseline (Panel A) to after the introduction of the new technology (Panel B). As expected, there are many conditions in our uncertainty parameter space under which the new program offers no benefits (red cells in Table 6.3). Importantly, however, even in those cases where attack C was preferred at baseline, the benefits of the new program are more than an order of magnitude lower than the $4 billion we calculated from our best estimate solution, because it failed to account for attack substitutions.

In addition to offering a simple and transparent method for explaining how risk reduction is likely to accrue from the introduction of new technology, the low-resolution model offers decisionmakers a candid assessment of how deep uncertainties affect the decision at hand. For instance, Panel C highlights that the new technology makes unequivocal sense only if we are designing it for terrorists with mid-range capabilities and only those who are not easily deterred by the risk of failure (green cells in Panel C). However, if we think terrorists view indirect economic effects as quite low (or, equivalently, they value these effects less than deaths and direct economic effects), then the program could also make sense for undeterable low-capability attackers or easily deterred high-capability attackers (yellow cells).

Which of these conditions represents a true depiction of current and future threats cannot be answered by the analyst with current data and information, so they should not be presented to decisionmakers as the single best judgment from bad data. Instead, the decisionmaker needs to understand what we know well, what we know poorly, and how the decision could be affected by uncertainty in the latter. The low-resolution model described here offers a means for communicating this information in a candid way (Requirement 5). Moreover, since the low-resolution model is supported by RMAT, TSSRA, and potentially other data sources, the analyst can offer the decisionmaker more detailed analysis on any assumptions the decisionmaker questions in the low-resolution model. If, for instance, the decisionmaker asks why the low-resolution model constrains the probabilities of success for attack A to be no higher than 0.50, the analyst might explain the RMAT analyses and any other considerations used to arrive at that value.

The transparency and face validity of such low-resolution models make them appropriate for supporting policy decisions (Requirement 20) and for communications with external stakeholders (Requirement 21). Finally, a clear attraction of this type of low-resolution model is that it can be easily implement in a spreadsheet, allowing analysts to evaluate multiple security options quickly (Requirements 22 and 23).

CHAPTER SEVEN

Conclusions

TSA policies and investment decisions require judgments that consider many competing interests, including effects on

- terrorism risk to the aviation system
- carrier and airport operations and costs
- the costs of implementing and maintaining the policy
- privacy, time burdens, and other concerns of travelers.

For considering the effects of new policies on system risk, TSA has several important resources, including a risk-management doctrine that recognizes many of the challenges of risk assessment when confronted with an adaptive adversary, such as many sources of deep uncertainty about the adversary's intentions, capabilities, and methods; the likelihood that counterterrorism measures may not eliminate risks so much as shift risk to different targets; and the likelihood that adversaries will develop tactics we have not anticipated (TSA, 2009b).

RMAT is one tool used by TSA to understand how its risk principles, intelligence estimates, and other information can be combined to provide quantitative estimates of the likely benefits of new policies or investments. Nevertheless, RMAT was not explicitly designed to implement current TSA risk doctrine and assumptions. Indeed, at the time RMAT was begun, TSA's approach to risk analysis and risk management was rudimentary. The process of developing RMAT led TSA to an increasingly sophisticated understanding of the nature of the threats, vulnerabilities, and possible consequences, as demonstrated in its current risk doctrine. As such, RMAT has served one of the objectives most often supported by complex simulations: It has improved understanding and insight into the nature of the phenomena it models. In this report, we have evaluated whether RMAT provides risk assessments that satisfy TSA's requirements and intended uses. Because RMAT was not designed to implement current TSA doctrine or requirements, nor were detailed requirements developed to guide its original development, we cannot assess whether RMAT meets its original objectives. Instead, we have considered whether any of TSA's current risk-assessment requirements can be satisfied by RMAT, and we find that RMAT does indeed fully satisfy five and partially satisfy 11 of the 19 high- and medium-priority requirements we identified.

In addition, we have examined how and whether RMAT could be used by TSA to support policy and resource allocation decisions. Our assessment is that there are appropriate uses that build on RMAT strengths but there are some weaknesses too that limit the utility of RMAT results for some of TSA's intended uses.

RMAT Key Strengths and Weaknesses for TSA Decision Support

RMAT is an ambitious attempt to model what is known about the decisionmaking process of potential adversaries as a way to anticipate current and future threats and terrorist adaptation to new security countermeasures. There are few general but detailed theories of terrorist behavior and decisionmaking on which to build such a model. RMAT has effectively developed such a theory, which could now serve to spur further refinements and elaboration by a wider community of analysts and academics. Similarly, in developing the RMAT tool, Boeing and TSA have identified many of the factors that might need to be understood before detailed models of terrorism risk can provide credible estimates. Clarification of these multiple influences on terrorism outcomes can also serve to highlight important sources of uncertainty for policymakers, to help subject matter experts provide more refined and precise judgments, and to focus intelligence analysts on important data that might otherwise go unnoticed.

Relatedly, RMAT represents an organized library of current estimates on each of these potentially important underlying phenomena. Even without executing a single RMAT run, the tool has value in consolidating intelligence information, technical reports, policies and procedure information, subject matter expert judgments, and other data sources on questions relevant to many models and policy questions. Assuming that the best available information has been supplied to RMAT, it can serve as a valuable resource for other modeling efforts, or when answering leadership questions about, for instance, what reasonable estimates of terrorist recruiting rates might be, how hard it is for terrorists to build different weapons, or related questions.

The RMAT model of the air transportation system is a particular strength. The current generalized air transportation system modeled in RMAT captures the key features relevant to security at most airports. If we have good information about an adversary's capabilities and intentions, the RMAT defender model can provide credible estimates of the likelihood that the adversary will be detected and interdicted. Moreover, modification of the defender model is straightforward, so to the extent that they fall within the scope of the RMAT "world," new places, processes, and vulnerabilities can be incorporated.

As discussed in this report, there are also important limitations on the valid use of RMAT results. We have highlighted, for instance, important limitations in the theory and data used by the RMAT adversary model, such as the assumption that terrorists are seeking to maximize expected monetized damages across deaths and direct and indirect economic effects; that they discount the importance of psychological or symbolic effects to a value of 0; that they do not consider the possibility that their attacks will trigger large one-time government costs associated with, for instance, the implementation of new security measures or military action; and that the model assumes more reconnaissance and dry runs on the part of adversaries than is reasonable.

In many cases, the problems identified with RMAT concern inaccuracies or imprecision in the model's input values, roughly 200 of which may be estimated incorrectly, rather than problems with the model's structure. One could argue that problems with input variables do not invalidate the model, per se, but instead highlight the need for improved data. However, to the extent RMAT has been designed to require unknowable or even very difficult-to-know parameters, this also reflects a challenge created by the model's design.

For instance, the model includes a parameter that can be used to quantify the psychological impact of attacks and another that allows the user to weight how importantly this parameter figures into the terrorist's decisionmaking. Because intangible psychological effects such as support for foreign policy objectives are extremely difficult to estimate and quantify, they have been set to 0. Nevertheless, the model is designed to require that such an estimate produce credible or even face-valid results.

Useful models require careful analysis of what we can and cannot know and then devising a strategy for cleverly addressing important sources of uncertainty. In the case of psychological effects, for instance, it may be that these cannot readily be monetized, so cannot be integrated into an overarching risk score expressed in terms of expected losses in dollars. Instead, it may be necessary to conceptualize intangible psychological effects as a separate dimension of risk. Similarly, inasmuch as quantitative estimates of psychological effects are subject to deep uncertainties, developers might explore strategies for illustrating how large differences in assumed psychological impacts might affect model results.

RMAT includes many variables that may be difficult or impossible to estimate with precision. Imprecise estimates on these variables may lead to model results that are completely wrong. In some cases, our sensitivity analyses revealed that these questionably knowable parameters exert a strong leverage over model results, as in the case of parameters describing terrorists' perception of the diminishing returns on additional parallel attacks, the parameters that dictates how rapidly the adversary can update his knowledge of security systems, and the parameters terrorists would apply to candidate attacks for purposes of judging their relative attractiveness. These and other RMAT parameters required by its design are subject to deep uncertainties, requiring information beyond what intelligence or academic research can credibly provide. Although TSA avoids some of these questionable parameters by using forced mode in RMAT, which relies more heavily on the defender portions of the model, our sensitivity analysis demonstrates that uncertain adversary characteristics continue to exert a powerful influence over model outcomes in forced mode.

As discussed in Chapter Six, the fact that many RMAT parameters, their distributions, and even the human and natural processes underlying the phenomena are subject to great uncertainty is itself an important caveat on the credibility of RMAT results. There is a temptation to believe that because each parameter has been estimated to the best of our subject matter experts' ability, the model results represent a best estimate as to how new policies or investments will perform in the future. Unfortunately, the presence of deep uncertainties make such best estimates poor ones on which to base policy decisions. By analogy, even if our best estimate is that the stock of one company will outperform the rest of the market, the presence of important sources of uncertainty in our judgment should cause us to seek an investment strategy that is likely to perform well across a range of possible future market conditions.

Our critique on this point is easily misunderstood, so we want to emphasize that we believe that many good and useful policy models require the inclusion of parameters that cannot be estimated with precision. It would be convenient if the world was simple enough to model adequately with highly knowable parameters, but this is rarely true. When these less knowable parameters are included in models, however, it is necessary to provide users with a comprehensive understanding of how uncertainties in the parameter values affect model results. Typically, this means evaluating a combination of values on each such parameter that span the range of plausible input conditions and then highlighting how regions in the spanning set of input conditions produce qualitatively different outcomes. This is not how the RMAT uncertain input values have been examined to date, and the seemingly large number of uncertain parameters may lead to a very large set of outcomes in any spanning set analysis that would strain analysts' efforts to make sense of.

TSA's risk doctrine emphasizes the importance of recognizing how deep uncertainties can affect estimates of future conditions, suggesting the need for TSA "to craft strategies that lessen our vulnerability to uncertainty and to our assumptions about the risks we face" (TSA, 2008a, p. 16). An important limitation of RMAT is that it cannot be easily configured to highlight the importance of deep uncertainties. As designed, it has many thousands of input variables, meaning that it is not appropriate for exploratory analysis that examines the entire parameter space. Moreover, it takes so long to run that neither Boeing nor RAND have been able to conduct even a superficial sensitivity analysis on all its variables to explore which parameters and assumptions may have the greatest influence on model outcomes. Instead, RMAT is most appropriate for generating point estimates of risk reduction implied by the joint effects of many thousands of assumptions and parameter estimates, an approach that can provide useful results about what could be true but which is less useful for understanding which outcomes are likely to occur.

As discussed in Chapter Six, another limitation on the usefulness of RMAT for decision support is the models' complexity. With thousands of input variables, assumptions, and caveats, RMAT cannot be viewed as having strong face validity, although some portions of the model, such as the defender model, clearly do have good face validity. Neither is it possible to attribute it with the external validity that might come from comparing RMAT predictions to empirical data on risk. As such, RMAT does not satisfy a general requirement of policy analysis models that they be transparent and intelligible (Bigelow and Davis, 2003), nor does it meet the TSA's own requirement for risk-management methodologies that are transparent (TSA, 2009b, p. 18) and can be used to communicate risk assessments with leadership, oversight, and stakeholder groups (Requirement 21).

In addition to these limitations of RMAT results, some of the ways RMAT is used can yield misleading findings or conclusions. In Chapter Six, for instance, we discussed how failure to use RMAT in the competition mode can lead to estimates of the probability of attack success that fail to properly account for risk-shifting. Whether decisionmakers can understand caveats about this kind of limitation, and mentally adjust RMAT results and the cost benefit analyses they support to account for risk-shifting, is questionable.

As a final limitation, we note that the RMAT software itself appears to be somewhat unstable, with errors detected and new updates to correct the errors occurring regularly through the course of our work with it. This is especially a concern, since the software architecture is not modularized in a way that makes error detection and testing easy or straightforward.

RMAT Validity

RMAT has proven to be of great value to TSA in driving a more sophisticated understanding of terrorism risks to the air transportation system. This is an example of the second class of uses we introduced in Chapter One, those designed to facilitate understanding of important phenomena and to record, structure, and convey information that is complex and not well understood. RMAT aides in structuring TSA's risk-analysis challenges and offers a repository of subject matter expert and other data on many factors of clear importance to TSA and security planning. As such, RMAT is like a textbook for TSA analysts and decisionmakers who must understand all of the details and ideas it describes to do their jobs well. RMAT is clearly valid for all these purposes.

As with all other terrorism risk models, it is not well suited for revealing how the future is likely to unfold. Even if the conceptual models on which RMAT is built were proven to be correct and comprehensive, the input data requirements exceed what subject matter experts or science can estimate with precision, and the imprecision of those estimates is subject to unknown sources and ranges of error. Because it cannot be relied on for such strongly predictive uses, its risk-reduction estimates for new technologies are of quite limited value for high-stakes decisionmaking: Those estimates might be good, or they they might be completely wrong, depending on factors we do not yet understand.

Finally, RMAT itself may not be well suited for the kinds of exploratory analysis required for high-stakes decision support, because of its reliance on such a large number of uncertain parameters and conceptual models, but it can and should be used for supporting development of a set of low-resolution models that can be used for exploratory analysis. These lower-resolution models can be used to explore the effects of uncertainty on decision outcomes but could explicitly reference the RMAT conceptual model or results. For example, decisionmakers, oversight organizations, or stakeholder groups reviewing low-resolution models are likely to question how their parameter values or ranges were established. The answer could be that the ranges reflect multiple sources of data, including judgments of experts, ranges observed across different RMAT runs, and other data. That is, RMAT insights into air transportation risk could be abstracted into low-resolution models that are better suited for exploratory analysis and simpler to explain and understand.

In addition, some components of RMAT, such as the simulated checkpoint, can provide deep and valid insights into the flow of passengers and the associated accumulation of risk under different sets of assumptions. We highlight the checkpoint, because risk here can be construed as a simpler accumulation of probabilistic events determined chiefly by TSA policies. Indeed, Boeing has created a stand-alone checkpoint emulator that offers a simple probabilistic risk model that could be used for this purpose. However, this tool was not a focus of this report.

In many ways, therefore, we are suggesting to TSA an idea very similar to one Francis Kapper offered to the Department of Defense three decades ago:

> The most appropriate and valid objectives for using war games and simulations within the DoD context are to: better understand complex phenomena, identify problems, evaluate alternatives, gain new insights, and broaden one's perspectives. The least valid or appropriate objectives for using war games and simulations are to predict combat/crisis outcomes or control broad and highly complex programs. (Hartley, 1997, p. 929)

Requirements for a TSA Risk Assessment

Table A.1
Requirements for a TSA Risk Assessment

No.	Priority	Description	Chapter
		Risk Modeling	
1	High	Risk estimation should be consistent with all TSA risk-assessment principles described in the TSA Risk Doctrine v1.1, July 2009, and TSA Risk Management Approach, December 2008.	6
2	High	Risk-reduction estimates for countermeasures should be calculated for a 5–10 year acquisition planning horizon, taking into account the evolution of defender systems.	6
3	High	Risk-assessment methods should specify risk as expected losses (L) over some period of time. For adversaries' probability of successful attack, A, and defender consequences given a successful attack, C, quantified as estimated number of deaths, direct economic damages, and indirect economic damages (factoring in resilience and psychological effects), the tool should calculate losses as L = A*C.	3
4	High	Risk-assessment methods should provide estimates of risk and the risk reduction attributable to individual countermeasures in terms of both absolute levels of risk and relative reductions in comparison to an established baseline.	6
5	High	Risk assessment should provide clear and accurate information about any uncertainties in its results as well as any dependence of the results on explicit or implicit assumptions.	6
6	Medium	Risk assessment should clarify the attack preferences of potential adversaries.	2
7	Low	Risk assessments should account for the deterrence effects of security countermeasures.	

Table A.1—Continued

No.	Priority	Description	Chapter
		Adversary Modeling	
8	High	Risk analyses should conceptualize adversaries as adaptive, assessing how risks to the air transportation system and its subsystems change as adversaries attempt to evade new or existing countermeasures or shift their attacks to alternative targets.	2
9	High	Risk analyses should represent the behavior of all potential adversaries (foreign and domestic; high- and low-skilled) using empirical evidence on such adversaries' behavior or widely accepted estimates of their behavior and capabilities.	2
		System Vulnerabilities	
10	High	The scope of air transportation risk assessments should be the U.S. commercial aviation system and those off-airport/off-aviation locations required to support adversarial planning. At a minimum, this should include any vulnerabilities at domestic airports associated with incoming international air cargo and passengers, the airport perimeter, aircraft maintenance, airside operations, domestic cargo, vehicle access control, security programs and instruments, passenger flow through the airport, airport threat alert status, passenger and employee credentialing, baggage identification, and key off-airport systems such as air traffic control, catering services, contractors, and vendors. Additional potential air system vulnerabilities, in descending order of priority, include international commercial airports, major differences between airports, general aviation air systems, mass transit systems at airports, cyber vulnerabilities (such as Air Traffic Control), and vulnerabilities unique to individual airports.	3
11	High	Risk assessments should address the aviation security threats and vulnerabilities detailed in TSSRA. They should include a range of potential insider attacks from airport employees and vendors, challenges to airport perimeter security, unauthorized access to secure airport areas, landside and airside attacks, chemical and biological threats, technological spoofing, and operational spoofing.	3
12	Low	Risk assessment should account for the possibility of unanticipated attack strategies by, for instance, assuming that security systems will never be able to lower system risk below some minimum level.	3

Table A.1—Continued

No.	Priority	Description	Chapter
		Security Systems	
13	High	In calculating risk, methods should account for security provided by TSA, carriers, airport operations, local law enforcement, and others' plans, programs, policies and procedures. Recognizing that countermeasure effects may be interdependent, risk assessments should be able to account for the joint effects of all security measures as these are implemented, modified, or planned by security providers, and the incremental effects of new security measures over the baseline risk offered by existing security systems.	3
14	High	Risk assessment should represent performance variations in security measures resulting from such factors as heterogeneity in officer performance (due to skill levels, attention, etc.), partial or incomplete deployment of security measures within or across airports, unreliability of technology systems or processes, or performance degradation due to passenger throughput, instrument calibration, or other known sources.	3
15	Low	The tool should account for the security benefits attributable to the initiatives of passengers, bystanders, and other non-adversaries.	
		Data Management	
16	High	Data inputs and outputs for risk-assessment methods should be in a common file format that is readable and editable by common office productivity software.	5
17	High	Risk-assessment methods should be maintained to incorporate salient changes to the aviation system, countermeasures, and threats. They should be sufficiently flexible to incorporate new information within two weeks of when it becomes available.	5
18	Medium	Analysts should be able to edit risk-assessment methods to alter adversary or aviation system characteristics, including the number and characteristics of airport facilities and security policies and procedures.	5
19	Medium	All data supporting risk assessments, including, but not limited to, that regarding threat, vulnerability, consequences, instruments, procedures, and the aviation system, should be authenticated and traceable.	4

Table A.1—Continued

No.	Priority	Description	Chapter
		Intended Use	
20	High	Risk assessments should provide TSA with estimates useful for supporting risk-informed investment decisions and efforts to prioritize alternative investments in countermeasures. Support of security allocation decisions across transportation modes would satisfy a low priority and would require that the tool's outputs be consistent with and comparable to risk estimates produced for other transportation modes.	6
21	High	Risk assessment should meet the standards of such oversight organizations as OMB, DHS, GAO, or Congress. As such, the methods should be sufficiently transparent that they can be explained to oversight organizations as well as external audiences, including the aviation community.	6
22	High	Risk assessment and its supporting analytic process should be able to support multiple risk-analysis case studies concurrently and quick turnaround analyses providing results within 14 days of problem formulation to assist TSA in mitigating emerging threats.	6
23	Low	Risk-assessment methods should be usable by program analysts in real time.	

Bibliography

Bastic, M., and A. Lovec, *Analysing the 11th September and Consequences: Final Report of the National Construction Safety Team on the Collapses of the World Trade Center Towers,* Gaithersburg, Md.: National Institute on Standards and Technology, 2005. As of July 30, 2012: http://wtc.nist.gov/NCSTAR1/NCSTAR1index.htm

Berrebi, Claude, "The Economics of Terrorism," in Paul K. Davis and Kim Cragin, eds., *Social Science for Counterterrorism: Putting the Pieces Together,* Santa Monica, Calif: RAND Corporation, MG-849-OSD, 2009. As of July 30, 2012: http://www.rand.org/pubs/monographs/MG849.html

Bigelow James H., and Paul K. Davis, *Implications for Model Validation of Multi-Resolution Multiperspective Modeling (MRMPM) and Exploratory Analysis,* Santa Monica, Calif.: RAND Corporation, MR-1750-AF, 2003. As of July 30, 2012: http://www.rand.org/pubs/monograph_reports/MR1750.html

Body, Howard, and Colin Marston, "The Peace Support Operations Model: Origins, Development, Philosophy and Use," *Journal of Defense Modeling and Simulation: Applications, Methodology, Technology,* Vol. 8, No. 2, April 2011, pp. 69–77.

Boeing Corporation, "Commercial Airplanes," undated. As of August 31, 2011: http://www.boeing.com/commercial/prices/index.html

———, "RMAT V&V, Feb. 23–24, 2011," briefing to RAND Corporation, Arlington, Va., 2011.

Bogen, K. T., and E. D. Jones, "Risks of Mortality and Morbidity from Worldwide Terrorism: 1968–2004," *Risk Analysis,* Vol. 26, No. 1, 2006, pp. 45–59.

Boyd, D., and S. G. Regulinski, *Characterizing Uncertainty in Technology Cost and Performance,* Menlo Park, Calif.: Decision Focus Incorporated, Project Number 1114, 1979.

Brandt, Patrick T., and Todd Sandler, "What Do Transnational Terrorists Target? Has It Changed? Are We Safer?" *Journal of Conflict Resolution,* Vol. 54, No. 2, April 2010, pp. 214–236.

Bureau of Transportation Statistics, "TransStats," Research and Innovative Technology Administration, undated-a. As of August 31, 2011: http://www.transtats.bts.gov/

————, "Air Cargo Summary Data," Research and Innovative Technology Administration, undated-b. As of August 31, 2011: http://www.bts.gov/programs/economics_and_finance/air_travel_price_index/html/annual.html

Carroll, Stephen J., Tom LaTourrette, Brian G. Chow, Gregory S. Jones, and Craig W. Martin, *Distribution of Losses from Large Terrorist Attacks Under the Terrorism Risk Insurance Act,* Santa Monica, Calif.: RAND Corporation, MG-427-CTRMP As of July 30, 2012: http://www.rand.org/pubs/monographs/MG427.html

Chaturvedi, R., S. Mellema, A. Chaturvedi, M. Mulpuri, and G. Pinczuk, "Continuous Validation Framework: A Case Study of SEAS and Afghanistan," Interservice/Industry Training, Simulation, and Education Conference (I/ITSEC), 2008. As of September 1, 2011: http://ntsa.metapress.com/link.asp?id=el32u127r54337j0

Cojazzi, G., D. Foglia, G. Grassinia, P. De Gelderb, D. Gryffroyb, R. Boladoc, E. Hoferd, R. Virolainene, I. M. Coef, A. Bassanellig, J. Pugah, I. Papazogloui, O. Zuchuatj, E. Cazzolik, J. Eyinkl, G. Guidam, L. Pinolaa, U. Pulkkinena, K. Simolan, D. von Winterfeldto, and A. Valeria, "Benchmark Exercise on Expert Judgment Techniques in PSA Level 2," *Nuclear Engineering and Design,* Vol. 209, No. 1–3, 2001, pp. 211–221.

Crenshaw, Martha, "Theories of Terrorism: Instrumental and Organizational Approaches," in David Rapoport, ed., *Inside Terrorist Organizations,* London: Frank Cass Publishers, 2001.

Cruickshank, Paul, and Mohannad Hage Ali, "Abu Musab Al Suri: Architect of the New Al-Qa'ida," *Studies in Conflict and Terrorism,* Vol. 30, No. 1, 2007.

Davis, Paul K., *Modeling of Soft Factors in the RAND Strategy Assessment System (RSAS),* Santa Monica, Calif.: RAND Corporation, P-7538, 1989. As of December 9, 2011: http://www.rand.org/pubs/papers/P7538.html

————, "A Framework for Verification, Validation, and Accreditation," in Adelia E. Ritchie, ed., *Simulation Validation Workshop Proceedings (SIMVAL II),* VI 1-39, Alexandria, Va.: Military Operations Research Society, 1992.

————, *Analytic Architecture for Capabilities-Based Planning, Mission-System Analysis, and Transformation,* Santa Monica, Calif.: RAND Corporation, MR-1513-OSD, 2002. As of August 15, 2007: http://www.rand.org/pubs/monograph_reports/MR1513.html

————, "Exploratory Analysis and Implications for Modeling," Chapter 9 in Stuart E. Johnson, Martin C. Libicki, and Gregory Treverton, eds., *New Challenges, New Tools for Defense Decisionmaking,* Santa Monica, Calif.: RAND Corporation, MR-1576-RC, 2003. As of July 30, 2012: http://www.rand.org/pubs/monograph_reports/MR1576.html

Davis, Paul K. and Kim Cragin, eds., *Social Science for Counterterrorism: Putting the Pieces Together,* Santa Monica, Calif.: RAND Corporation, MG-849-OSD, 2009. As of July 15, 2011: http://www.rand.org/pubs/monographs/MG849.html

Davis, Paul K., and Amy Henninger, *Analysis, Analysis Practices, and Implications for Modeling and Simulation,* Santa Monica, Calif.: RAND Corporation, OP-176-OSD, 2007. As of July 30, 2012: http://www.rand.org/pubs/occasional_papers/OP176.html

Davis, Paul K., Jonathan Kulick, and Michael Egner, *Implications of Modern Decision Science for Military Decision-Support Systems,* Santa Monica, Calif.: RAND Corporation, MG-360-AF, 2005. As of July 30, 2012: http://www.rand.org/pubs/monographs/MG360.html

Davis, Paul K., R. D. Shaver, and Justin Beck, *Portfolio-Analysis Methods for Assessing Capability Options,* Santa Monica, Calif.: RAND Corporation, MG-662-OSD, 2008. As of July 30, 2012: http://www.rand.org/pubs/monographs/MG662.html

Department of Defense, *Quadrennial Defense Review,* 2009.

————, "Minerva Research Initiative (MRI)," program announcement, Federal Triangle Park, N.C., July 2011. As of July 27, 2011: http://www.arl.army.mil/www/pages/8/research/Minerva_Draft_BAA_Final_July2011.pdf

Department of Homeland Security, *National Infrastructure Protection Plan,* 2009, Washington, D.C.

Dewar, James A., Steven C. Bankes, James S. Hodges, Thomas W. Lucas, Desmond Saunders-Newton, and Patrick Vye, *Credible Uses of the Distributed Interactive Simulation (DIS) System,* Santa Monica, Calif.: RAND Corporation, MR-607-A, 1996. As of July 30, 2012: http://www.rand.org/pubs/monograph_reports/MR607.html

Dewar, James A., Carl H. Builder, William M. Hix, and Morlie H. Levin, *Assumption-Based Planning: A Planning Tool for Very Uncertain Times,* Santa Monica, Calif.: RAND Corporation, MR-114-A, 1993. As of July 30, 2012: http://www.rand.org/pubs/monograph_reports/MR114.html

DoD—*See* Department of Defense.

Drake, C. J. M., "The Role of Ideology in Terrorists' Target Selection," *Terrorism and Political Violence,* Vol. 10, No. 2, 1998.

Electronic Code of Federal Regulations, "Foreign Air Carrier Security," Title 49, Part 1546, undated. As of August 31, 2011:
http://ecfr.gpoaccess.gov/cgi/t/text/text-idx?c=ecfr&sid= 2940ff80be1e46634f6deadcc8f79dbe&rgn=div5&view=text&node= 49:9.1.3.5.13&idno=49

Enders, W., "Terrorism: An Empirical Analysis," in K. Hartley and T. Sandler, eds., *Handbook of Defense Economics: Defense in a Globalized World*, Vol. 2, Amsterdam: North Holland, 2007.

Enders, Walter, and Todd Sandler, "The Effectiveness of Anti-Terrorism Policies: A Vector-Autoregression-Intervention Analysis," *American Political Science Review*, Vol. 87, No. 4, 1993.

―――, "Patterns of Transnational Terrorism, 1970–1999: Alternative Time Series Estimates," *International Studies Quarterly*, Vol. 46, 2002, pp. 145–165.

Enders, Walter, and Xuejuan Su, "Rational Terrorists and Optimal Network Structure," *Journal of Conflict Resolution*, Vol. 51, No. 1, 2007.

Florig, H. Keith, M. Granger Morgan, Kara M. Morgan, Karen E. Jenni, Baruch Fischhoff, Paul S. Fischbeck, and Michael L. DeKay, "A Deliberative Method for Ranking Risks (I): Overview and Test Bed Development," *Risk Analysis*, Vol. 21, No. 5, 2001, pp. 913–921.

Frey, B. S., S. Luechinger, and A. Stutzer, "Calculating Tragedy: Assessing the Costs of Terrorism," *Journal of Economic Surveys*, Vol. 21, No. 1, 2007, pp. 1–24

Galway, Lionel A., *Subjective Probability Distribution Elicitation in Cost Risk Analysis: A Review*, Santa Monica, Calif.: RAND Corporation, TR-410-AF, 2007. As of July 15, 2011:
http://www.rand.org/pubs/technical_reports/TR410.html

GAO—*See* U.S. Government Accountability Office.

Goldberg, Jeffrey, "The Things He Carried," *The Atlantic*, November 2008.

Gordon, P., J. E. Moore, II, J. Y. Park, and H. W. Richardson, "The Economic Impacts of a Terrorist Attack on the U.S. Commercial Aviation System," *Risk Analysis*, Vol. 27, No. 3, 2007, pp. 505–512.

Groves, David G., and Robert J. Lempert, *A New Analytic Method for Finding Policy-Relevant Scenarios*, Santa Monica, Calif.: RAND Corporation, RP-1244, 2007. As of July 30, 2012:
http://www.rand.org/pubs/reprints/RP1244.html

Gustafson, David H., Ramesh K. Shukla, Andre Delbecq, and G. William Walster, "A Comparative Study of Differences in Subjective Likelihood Estimates Made by Individuals, Interacting Groups, Delphi Groups, and Nominal Groups," *Organizational Behavior and Human Performance*, Vol. 9, No. 2, April 1973, pp. 200–291.

Hartley, D. S., "Verification and Validation in Military Simulations," in S. Andradottir, K. J. Healy, D.H.S. Withers, and B. L. Nelson, eds., *Proceedings of the 1997 Winter Simulation Conference,* 1997.

———, *VV&A for DIME/PMESII Models,* 2008. As of August 30, 2011: http://www.ndu.edu/CTNSP/docUploaded/HSCB%20Hartley%20-%20VVA%20Group%20-%20Final%20Version.doc

Helfstein, Scott, and Dominick Wright, "Success, Lethality, and Cell Structure Across the Dimensions of Al-Qa'ida," *Studies in Conflict and Terrorism,* Vol. 34, No. 5, 2011.

Hiss, J., and T. Kahana,"Suicide Bombers in Israel," *American Journal of Forensic Medicine and Pathology,* Vol. 19, 1998, pp. 63–66.

Hodges, James S., "Six or So Things You Can Do with a Bad Model," *Operations Research,* Vol. 29, 1991, pp. 355–365.

Hodges, James S., and James A. Dewar, *Is It You or Your Model Talking? A Framework for Model Validation,* Santa Monica, Calif.: RAND Corporation, R-4114-AF/A/OSD, 1992. As of July 30, 2012: http://www.rand.org/pubs/reports/R4114.html

Homeland Security Institute, "Risk Management Analysis Process (RMAP): Quick Look Analysis Final Briefing," Washington, D.C., December 18, 2006.

———, "Underlying Reasons for Success and Failure of Terrorist Attacks," June 4, 2007. As of August 30, 2011: http://www.homelandsecurity.org/hsireports/reasons_for_terrorist_success_failure.pdf

Hora, Stephen C., "Eliciting Probabilities from Experts," in Ward Edwards, Ralph F. Miles, Jr., and Detiof von Winterfeldt, eds., *Advances in Decision Analysis: From Foundations to Applications,* Cambridge, U.K.: Cambridge University Press, 2007a.

———, "Expert Judgment, in Advances in Decision Analysis: From Foundations to Applications," in Ward Edwards, Ralph F. Miles, Jr., and Detiof von Winterfeldt, eds., *Advances in Decision Analysis: From Foundations to Applications,* Cambridge, U.K.: Cambridge University Press, 2007b.

HSI—*See* Homeland Security Institute.

Jackson, Brian, "Groups, Networks, or Movements: A Command-and-Control-Driven Approach to Classifying Terrorist Organizations and Its Application to Al-Qa'ida," *Studies in Conflict and Terrorism,* Vol. 29, No. 3, 2006.

———, "Organizational Decisionmaking by Terrorist Groups," in Paul K. Davis and Kim Cragin, eds., *Social Science for Counterterrorism: Putting the Pieces Together,* Santa Monica, Calif.: RAND Corporation, MG-849-OSD, 2009. As of July 15, 2011: http://www.rand.org/pubs/monographs/MG849.html

Jackson, Brian A., and David R. Frelinger, *Understanding Why Terrorist Operations Succeed or Fail,* Santa Monica, Calif.: RAND Corporation, OP-257-RC, 2009. As of July 15, 2011:
http://www.rand.org/pubs/occasional_papers/OP257.html

———, "The Problem to Be Solved: Historical, Contemporary, and Future Threats to Aviation Security," in Brian A. Jackson, Tom LaTourrette, Edward W. Chan, Russell Lundberg, Andrew R. Morral, and David R. Frelinger, eds., *Efficient Aviation Security: Strengthening the Analytic Foundation for Making Air Transportation Security Decisions,* Santa Monica, Calif.: RAND Corporation, MG-1220-RC, 2012. As of September 18, 2012:
http://www.rand.org/pubs/monographs/MG1220.html

Jackson, Brian A., Peter Chalk, Kim Cragin, Bruce Newsome, John Parachini, William Rosenau, Erin M. Simpson, Melanie W. Sisson, and Donald Temple, *Breaching the Fortress Wall: Understanding Terrorist Efforts to Overcome Defensive Technologies,* Santa Monica, Calif.: RAND Corporation, MG-481-DHS, 2007. As of July 30, 2012:
http://www.rand.org/pubs/monographs/MG481.html

Japan Airlines, "Safety Operations," undated. As of August 31, 2011:
http://www.jal.com/en/safety/airport/

Jenkins, Brian, "Defense Against Terrorism," *Political Science Quarterly,* Vol. 101, No. 5, 1986.

Jordan, Javier, Fernando M. Mañas, and Nicola Horsburgh, "Strengths and Weaknesses of Grassroots Jihadist Networks: The Madrid Bombings," *Studies in Conflict and Terrorism,* Vol. 31, No. 1, 2008.

Kazda, Antonin, and Robert E. Caves, *Airport Design and Operation,* Oxford, U.K.: Elsevier Science, 2007.

Kenney, Michael, "Dumb Yet Deadly: Local Knowledge and Poor Tradecraft Among Islamists Militants in Britain and Spain," *Studies in Conflict and Terrorism,* Vol. 33, No. 10, 2010.

Korol, Matt, "Measuring the Impact of 9/11 on US Airline Enplanements," The Boeing Company, October 2008.

LaTourrette, Tom, David R. Howell, David E. Mosher, and John M. MacDonald, *Reducing Terrorism Risk at Shopping Centers: An Analysis of Potential Security Options,* Santa Monica, Calif.: RAND Corporation, TR-401, 2006. As of July 30, 2012:
http://www.rand.org/pubs/technical_reports/TR401.html

Lempert, Robert J., and Michael E. Schlesinger, "Robust Strategies for Abating Climate Change," *Climatic Change,* Vol. 45, 2000, pp. 387–401.

Lempert, Robert J., Steven W. Popper, and Steven C. Bankes, *Shaping the Next One Hundred Years: New Methods for Quantitative Long-Term Policy Analysis,* Santa Monica, Calif.: RAND Corporation, MR-1626-CR, 2003. As of July 30, 2012: http://www.rand.org/pubs/monograph_reports/MR1626.html

Lempert, Robert J., Michael E. Schlesinger, and Stephen C. Bankes, "When We Don't Know the Costs or the Benefits: Adaptive Strategies for Abating Climate Change," *Climatic Change,* Vol. 33, 1996, pp. 235–274.

Libicki, Martin C., Peter Chalk, and Melanie W. Sisson, *Exploring Terrorist Targeting Preferences,* Santa Monica, Calif.: RAND Corporation, MG-483-DHS, 2007. As of July 30, 2012: http://www.rand.org/pubs/monographs/MG483.html

Lichtblau, Eric, "The Plot: Bin Ladin Chose 9/11 Targets, Al-Qa'ida Leader Says," *The New York Times,* March 20, 2003.

Linstone, Harold, and Murray Turoff, *The Delphi Method: Techniques and Applications,* Reading, Mass.: Addison-Wesley, 1975.

McCartan, Lisa M., Andrea Masselli, Michael Rey, and Danielle Rusnak, "The Logic of Terrorist Target Choice: An Examination of Chechen Rebel Bombings from 1997–2003," *Studies in Conflict and Terrorism,* Vol. 31, No. 1, 2008.

McConnell, Michael J., Director of National Intelligence, "Intelligence Community Directive No. 203," Washington, D.C., June 17, 2007. As of July 30, 2012: http://www.fas.org/irp/dni/icd/icd-203.pdf

Mlakar, Paul E., Donald O. Dusenberry, James R. Harris, Gerald Haynes, Long T. Phan, and Mete A. Sozen, *The Pentagon Building Performance Report,* Reston, Va.: American Society of Civil Engineers, January 2003. As of July 2012: http://www.asce.org/Product.aspx?ID=2147485891

Morgan, Kara M., Michael L. DeKay, Paul S. Fischbeck, M. Granger Morgan, Baruch Fischhoff, and H. Keith Florig, "A Deliberative Method for Ranking Risks (II): Evaluation of Validity and Agreement Among Risk Managers," *Risk Analysis,* Vol. 21, No. 5, 2001, pp. 923–937.

Morgan, M. Granger, and Max Henrion, *Uncertainty: A Guide to Dealing with Uncertainty in Quantitative Risk and Policy Analysis,* Cambridge, U.K.: Cambridge University Press, 1990.

Morgan, M. Granger, Samual C. Morris, Max Henrion, Deborah A. L. Amaral, and William R. Rish, "Technical Uncertainty in Quantitative Policy Analysis: A Sulfur Air Pollution Example," *Risk Analysis,* Vol. 4, No. 3, September 1984, pp. 201–216.

Morral, Andrew R., and Brian A. Jackson, *Understanding the Role of Deterrence in Counterterrorism Security*, Santa Monica, Calif.: RAND Corporation, OP-281-RC, 2009. As of July 15, 2011:
http://www.rand.org/pubs/occasional_papers/OP281.html

Mueller, John, and Mark G. Stewart, *Terror, Security, and Money: Balancing the Risks, Benefits and Costs of Homeland Security*, Prepared for Presentation at the Panel, "Terror and the Economy: Which Institutions Help Mitigate the Damage?" at the Annual Convention of the Midwest Political Science Association, Chicago, Ill., April 1, 2011.

Myers, David G., and Helmut Lamm, "The Polarizing Effect of Group Discussions," *American Scientist*, Vol. 63, No. 3, 1975, pp. 297–303.

National Research Council, *Modeling and Simulation*, Volume 8, Technology for the 21st Century Navy and Marine Corps, Naval Studies Board, National Academy Press, Washington, D.C., 1997.

———, *Department of Homeland Security Bioterrorism Risk Assessment: A Call for Change*, Washington, D.C.: National Academies Press, 2008.

———, *Review of the Department of Homeland Security's Approach to Risk Analysis*, Washington, D.C.: National Academies Press, 2010.

NRC—*See* National Research Council.

Office of the Director of National Intelligence, Intelligence Community Directive, Number 203, *Analytic Standards*, Effective June 21, 2007. As of September 10, 2012:
http://www.fas.org/irp/dni/icd/icd-203.pdf

Office of Management and Budget, "Circular A-4," 2003. As of July 30, 2012:
http://www.whitehouse.gov/omb/circulars_a004_a-4/

Office of Naval Research, "HSCB Thrust," 2011. As of July 27, 2011:
http://www.onr.navy.mil/Science-Technology/Departments/Code-30/All-Programs/Human-Behavioral-Sciences.aspx

Pace, Dale K., "Modeling and Simulation Verification and Validation Challenges," *Johns Hopkins APL Technical Digest*, Vol. 25, No. 2, 2004. As of July 30, 2012:
http://www.jhuapl.edu/techdigest/TD/td2502/Pace.pdf

Peterson, R. M., R. H. Bittel, C. A. Forgie, W. H. Lee, and J. J. Nestor, "Using USCAP's Analytical Models, the Transportation Security Administration Balances the Impacts of Aviation Security Policies on Passengers and Airlines," *Interfaces*, Vol. 37, No. 1, 2007, pp. 52–67.

Pfleeger, Shari Lawrence, and Joanne M. Atlee, *Software Engineering: Theory and Practice*, 3rd ed., Upper Saddle River, N.J.: Pearson Prentice Hall, 2006.

Phillips, C. L., J. R. Crosscope, and N. D. Geddes, "Bayesian Modeling Using Belief Networks of Perceived Threat Levels Affected by Stratagemical Behavior Patterns," *Proceedings of the Second International Conference on Computational Cultural Dynamics*, 2008, pp. 55–64.

Pittel, K., and D. T. G. Rubbelke, "What Directs a Terrorist?" *Defence and Peace Economics*, Vol. 17, 2006, pp. 311–328.

Riley, Kevin Jack, *Air Travel Security Since 9/11*, Santa Monica, Calif.: RAND Corporation, CP-635, 2011. As of July 30, 2012:
http://www.rand.org/pubs/corporate_pubs/CP635.html

Ritchie, Adelia E., ed., *Simulation Validation Workshop Proceedings (SIMVAL II)*, Alexandria, Va.: Military Operations Research Society, 1992.

Robinson, L. A., J. K. Hammitt, J. E. Aldy, A. Krupnick, and J. Baxter, "Valuing the Risk of Death from Terrorist Attacks," *Journal of Homeland Security and Emergency Management*, Vol. 7, No. 1, 2010, pp. 1–25.

Rose, Adam Z., Gbadebo Oladosu, Bumsoo Lee, and Garrett R. Beeler Asay, "The Economic Impacts of the September 11 Terrorist Attacks: A Computable General Equilibrium Analysis," *Published Articles & Papers*, Paper 67, 2009. As of September 18, 2012:
http://research.create.usc.edu/published_papers/67

Sandler, T., and W. Enders, "Economic Consequences of Terrorism in Developed and Developing Countries: An Overview," in P. Keefer and N. Loayza, eds., *Terrorism, Economic Development, and Political Openness*, Cambridge, U.K.: Cambridge University Press, 2008, pp. 17–47.

Sandler, T., and J. L. Scott, "Terrorist Success in Hostage-Taking Incidents: An Empirical Study," *Journal of Conflict Resolution*, Vol. 31, 1987, pp. 35–53.

Sargent, R. G., "Validation and Verification of Simulation Models," in M. E. Kuhl, N. M. Steiger, F. B. Armstrong, and J. A. Joines, eds., *Proceedings of the 2005 Winter Simulation Conference*, 2005, pp. 130–143.

Schwartz, Peter, *The Art of the Long View*, New York: Doubleday, 1996.

Shughart, William, II, "An Analytic History of Terrorism, 1945–2000," *Public Choice*, Vol. 128, No. 1–2, 2006.

Slaughter, Richard, *The Knowledge Base of Futures Studies: Pro Edition (CD_ROM)*, 2005.

Slovic, P., "Perception of Risk," *Science*, Vol. 236, No. 4799, 1987, pp. 280–285.

Stoller, G., "Airport Security Breaches Since 2001 Raise Alarms," *USA Today*, July 13, 2011. As of July 30, 2012:
http://travel.usatoday.com/flights/story/2011/07/Airport-security-breaches-since-2001-raise-alarms/49326312/1

Transportation Research Board, *Airport Passenger Terminal Planning and Design,* Volume 1: *Guidebook,* Airport Cooperative Research Program Report 25, 2010. As of July 30, 2012:
http://www.trb.org/Publications/Blurbs/Airport_Passenger_Terminal_Planning_and_Design_Vol_163252.aspx

Transportation Security Administration, *Risk Assessment and Capabilities Design,* Washington, D.C., undated-a.

————, "Risk Management Analysis Process (RMAP)," Washington, D.C., undated-b (file: RMAP Overview_V6.docx).

————, "49 CFR, Subchapter C—Civil Aviation Security: Security Regulations," Washington, D.C., undated-c. As of September 1, 2011:
http://www.tsa.gov/research/laws/regs/editorial_multi_image_with_table_0203.shtm

————, "Global Strategies," Washington, D.C., undated-d. As of August 31, 2011:
http://www.tsa.gov/approach/harmonization.shtm as of August 31, 2011

————, "TSA Travel Assistant," Washington, D.C., undated-e. As of August 31, 2011:
http://www.tsa.gov/travelers/airtravel/screening/index.shtm#3

————, *Recommended Security Guidelines for Airport Planning, Design, and Construction,* Washington, D.C., 2006a. As of July 30, 2012:
http://www.tsa.gov/assets/pdf/airport_security_design_guidelines.pdf

————, *Security Checkpoint Layout Design/Reconfiguration Guide,* Washington, D.C., 2006b. As of July 30, 2012:
http://aci-na.org/static/entransit/Checkpoint_Layout_Design_Guide_v1r0-0.pdf

————, *TSA Risk Management Approach,* Washington, D.C., December 1, 2008a.

————, *Screening Management Standard Operating Procedures,* Washington, D.C., 2008b.

————, *Risk Assessment and Capabilities Design,* Washington, D.C., September 2009a.

————, *TSA Risk Doctrine,* Washington, D.C., July 14, 2009b.

————, *Checkpoint Design Guide (CDG) Revision 1,* Washington, D.C., 2009c. As of July 30, 2012:
http://www.aci-na.org/static/entransit/OPT Checkpoint Design Guide (CDG) 2009.pdf

————, *Transportation Sector Security Assessment,* Department of Homeland Security, Washington, D.C., March 2010.

———, *Recommended Security Guidelines for Airport Planning, Design, and Construction,* Washington, D.C., 2011. As of July 30, 2012:
http://www.tsa.gov/assets/pdf/airport_security_design_guidelines.pdf

Transportation Security Administration, Office of Security, Requirements *Document for the Risk Management Analysis Process (RMAP) Tool,* Washington, D.C., November 2009.

TSA—*See* Transportation Security Administration.

TSA-Sec—*See* Transportation Security Administration, Office of Security.

Tversky, Amos, and Daniel Kahneman, "Judgment under Uncertainty: Heuristics and Biases," *Science,* Vol. 185, No. 4157, September 27, 1974, pp. 1124–1131.

U.S. Government Accountability Office, *Review of Studies of the Economic Impact of the September 11, 2001, Terrorist Attacks on the World Trade Center,* Washington, D.C., GAO-02-700R, 2002. As of July 30, 2012:
http://www.gao.gov/new.items/d02700r.pdf

———, *Aviation Security: Foreign Airport Assessments and Air Carrier Inspections Help Enhance Security, but Oversight of These Efforts Can Be Strengthened,* Washington, D.C, GAO-07-729, 2007. As of July 30, 2012:
http://www.gao.gov/new.items/d07729.pdf

———, *Transportation Security: Comprehensive Risk Assessments and Stronger Internal Controls Needed to Help Inform TSA Resource Allocation,* Washington, D.C., GAO-09-492, March 2009. As of July 30, 2012:
http://www.gao.gov/new.items/d09492.pdf

———, *Aviation Security: TSA Is Increasing Procurement and Deployment of the Advanced Imaging Technology, but Challenges to This Effort and Other Areas of Aviation Security Remain,* Washington, D.C., GAO-10-484T, 2010a. As of July 30, 2012:
http://www.gao.gov/products/GAO-10-484T

———, *Aviation Security: Efforts to Validate TSA's Passenger Screening Behavior Detection Program Underway, but Opportunities Exist to Strengthen Validation and Address Operational Challenges,* Washington, D.C., GAO-10-763, 2010b. As of July 30, 2012:
http://www.gao.gov/products/GAO-10-763

———, *TSA Has Taken Steps to Enhance Its Foreign Airport Assessments, but Opportunities Exist to Strengthen the Program,* Washington, D.C., GAO-12-163, 2011. As of September 10, 2012:
http://www.gao.gov/products/GAO-12-163

UPS, "Air Freight: Within and Between Canada, the U.S. and Puerto Rico," 2011. As of August 31, 2011:
http://www.ups.com/media/en/ca/af_zones_rates_upc.pdf

Viscusi, W. K., "The Lulling Effect: The Impact of Child-Resistant Packaging on Aspirin and Analgesic Ingestions," *The American Economic Review*, Vol. 74, No. 2, Papers and Proceedings of the Ninety-Sixth Annual Meeting of the American Economic Association, May 1984, pp. 324–327.

———, "How to Value a Life," *Journal of Economics and Finance*, Vol. 32, 2008, pp. 311–323.

———, "Valuing Risks of Death from Terrorism and Natural Disasters," *Journal of Risk and Uncertainty*, Vol. 38, 2009, pp. 191–213.

Wallsten, T. S., and R. G. Whitfield, *Assessing the Risks to Young Children of Three Effects Associated with Elevated Blood-Lead Levels*, Argonne, Ill.: Argonne National Laboratory, ANL/AA-32, 1986.

Willis, H. H., and T. LaTourrette, "Using Probabilistic Terrorism Risk Modeling for Regulatory Benefit-Cost Analysis: Application to the Western Hemisphere Travel Initiative in the Land Environment," *Risk Analysis*, Vol. 28, 2008, pp. 325–329. As of July 30, 2012:
http://onlinelibrary.wiley.com/doi/10.1111/j.1539-6924.2008.01022.x/abstract

Willis, Henry H., and R. Lundberg, "Setting Priorities for Protecting Transportation Systems: Comparing Risks from Accidents, Disasters and Terrorism," paper presented at the Department of Homeland Security University Programs Summit, Washington, D.C., April 1, 2011.

Willis, Henry H., Michael L. DeKay, M. Granger Morgan, H. Keith Florig, and Paul S. Fischbeck, "Ecological Risk Ranking: Evaluation of a Method for Improving the Quality of Public Participation in Environmental Decision Making," *Risk Analysis*, Vol. 24, No. 2, 2004, pp. 363–378.

Willis, Henry H., Jacqueline MacDonald Gibson, Regina A. Shih, Sandra Geschwind, Sarah Olmstead, Jianhui Hu, Aimee E. Curtright, Gary Cecchine, and Melinda Moore, "Prioritizing Environmental Health Risks in the UAE," *Risk Analysis*, Vol. 20, No. 12, 2010, pp. 1842–1856.

Wilson, Jeremy M., Brian A. Jackson, Mel Eisman, Paul Steinberg, and Kevin Jack Riley, *Securing America's Passenger-Rail Systems*, Santa Monica, Calif.: RAND Corporation, MG-705-NIJ, 2007. As of July 30, 2012:
http://www.rand.org/pubs/monographs/MG705.html